DRAMA & DIPLOMACY

DRAMA & DIPLOMACY

J. McGill

MCGILL BOOKS

Puerto Vallarta, *Jalisco*

ACKNOWLEDGEMENTS

To the man who always believed I would...

...and to all of you who have touched our lives.

Also my deepest appreciation goes to my editors, the wonderfully wicked wise-cracking wizard of Mexconnect, who badgered me constantly and threatened to report me to the CIA for withholding pertinent information when I first balked at publishing this book, **Carol Wheeler, Senior Editor, Mexconnect**.

And I can't forget one of my DOMs ("Dirty", but Dear Old Men) in my life whose words of praise, encouragement, and gentle, but firm guidance caused me to visit the dressmaker for hem adjustments several times. "Walk tall, daughter!" is a big order for a runt like me. This second edition would never have come about if not for you, Billy Joe aka **William Reed**, historian and author of **Mexican Odyssey** and **Rocks & Shoals**.

"You never appreciate Old Glory until you see her flying from a palm thatched roof in a foreign country."
—**Alden "Mac" McMurtry**
October 31, 1905 – April 1, 2004

Drama & Diplomacy

For many of us living in the Guadalajara area, years may have passed since Puerto Vallarta held quirky small-town Mexican charm. Jenny McGill's "Drama and Diplomacy," an autobiographical work about her years as consular agent in the nascent beach resort, could help a few cynics see it (or at least its past) from a fresh perspective. Fortunately, it's also a perspective riddled with a healthy dose of humor ... Some say that you can't put down a good book. "Drama and Diplomacy" has something different in mind: short, readable vignettes, clearly separated, welcoming a bookmark until the next peaceful interlude and the next drink in the garden or on the couch ... McGill wields it well, painting a sympathetic, nostalgic portrait of Puerto Vallarta as it will never be again. The added bonus: a whole lot of juicy, zany gossip on some of the strangest gringos in the city's history ... The tales (which the author swears are all true) are amusing enough to entertain anyone new to the Vallarta scene, but will probably leave many old-timers cackling with laughter, rolling on the ground and clutching their stomach ... . This may be one of the most readable personal accounts of the mysterious and "glamorous" work of consular agents abroad.

—**Alex Gesheva**, *Colony Reporter,* **Guadalajara, Mexico**

I like this book … Jenny McGill and her husband Howard moved to Vallarta in the early '70s … These were good years to be in Vallarta, and during most of these years Jenny worked as a Consular Agent for the U.S. State Department. She was not involved in "diplomacy" but in the day to day grind, at a very human level, handling duties that were sometimes disgusting, sometimes heart-warming, sometimes even inspirational, often funny … Now Jenny and her husband Howard live in the pine-covered mountains of Talpa de Allende, home to only a handful of Americans. Many readers of *Mexico Connect* have discovered Jenny's series, nine pieces so far - *At Home in Talpa de Allende, Jalisco*. Charming, sometimes informative, sometimes sad, often touching, these are stories about life in the little community she now calls her home … so very different from her Puerto Vallarta, the "Sultry Mexican Beach Town" that provided her with so many tales to entertain us, her fascinated readers.

—**James Tipton**, *Mexico Connect Magazine*, **Guadalajara**, **Mexico**

Yes, there they were—many of them—the characters in former U.S. Consular Agent's Jenny McGill's new book that's receiving rave reviews all over Vallarta and beyond. The book, 'DRAMA & DIPLOMACY in a Sultry Mexican Beach Town,' has been invading bedside tables and lounge chairs around town as well as jumping into suitcases for travel reading since its appearance a few weeks ago. But it was the people IN the book who arrived at Burt Hixson and Gerry Battle's Villa Verano on Tuesday, 22 May to celebrate Jenny's triumph … Tables were draped with red, white and green and red, white and blue banners and Jenny, selling and signing her books was assisted by her Guadalajara friend Carol Wheeler, editor in chief of the online site MexConnect, Sally Conley of the Children's Library in Pitillal and Laura Cardenas of "I Do Vallarta." … And, as they say, many, many more … The book is a great, lively read … Angela Corelis, Judith Ewing Morlan and husband Ed and many, many more have registered solid thumbs up reviews as do I!

—**Barbara Sands**, *Vallarta Today* **Newspaper**

Jenny McGill's book is a series of biographical vignettes glimpsing into Puerto Vallarta's growth and history from the early 1970s to the mid-1990s ... There are a couple of murders of American citizens as well as episodes involving Mexican "brujas" or female witch doctors which makes this book hard to lay aside. Sex and humor are not lacking, as Jenny, a self-described "bureaucrap," meets with hilarity in places you'd least expect it ... Jenny sums it up: "My love of robin-egg blue skies, breath-taking sunsets that only God could paint, and music which falls softly on my ear, is reason enough to be in Mexico." The gamut of all of us ex-pats who have lived in late 20th century Puerto Vallarta makes its appearance in *Drama And Diplomacy In A Sultry Mexican Beach Town*

—Thomas Halley, El Ojo del Lago, Chapala, Mexico

Ambrose Bierce did not define Drama in his *Devil's Dictionary,* but if he had he would probably have defined it as: Unbelievable Events which are Absolutely True. *Exempli gratia:* A Mexican *novela* Soap Opera.

And that's what Jenny McGill's *Drama & Diplomacy in a Sultry Mexican Beach Town* reads like. Many descriptions come to mind: Tight-Tough; Mean-Lean; Sad-Sorrowful; Surrealistic-Realistic; Happy-Hilarious – which all add up to an absolutely-delightful reading experience. Try to imagine a composite painting by Diego Rivera, Pablo Picasso, Frederic Remington and Manuel Lepe – laid on with a bold brush which neither falters nor blushes – and you have a perfect image of this honest and touching work by former U.S. Consular Agent Jenny McGill. How refreshing to read something by a diplomat which rings of Truth! This book is a must read for anyone with the slightest interest in Puerto Vallarta – or for that matter, for anyone who just loves to cry and laugh a lot.

—William Reed, Garces Books, Puerto, Vallarta, Mexico

"She pulls no punches."
—B. Little, Modesto, CA

"Jenny McGill is a wonderfully wicked lady."
—C. Wheeler, Guadalajara

"She took dead aim and created a zipper of bullet holes from his navel to his crotch."
— H. McGill

"My laptop is going to rust from the tears of laughter."
—B. Hixson, Puerto Vallarta

"It reads like she is sitting on the terrace with you sipping margaritas."
—G. Battle, Puerto Vallarta

"Enjoyed the book and very proud of you, Sis."
—P. Flanery, Puerto Vallarta

"I bought the book the minute I saw it in Rizo's. My jaws haven't stopped hurting yet from laughing. Well done and congratulations!"
—R. Dry, Puerto Vallarta

"Your life was the sort that people would think, 'Don't bother writing about it. Nobody would believe it!' Drama & Diplomacy is believable and rings of the truth."
—E. Harris, Puerto Vallarta

"Glad to see when you retired you could publish the truth. We are enjoying the book in Guadalajara"
—R. Walker, Guadalajara

"We want to come to all your book signings. We can read about our past lives in the book."
—S. Love, Puerto Vallarta

" AJUAA!"

—B. Sands, Puerto Vallarta

'Can't tell you how much I'm enjoying your book, all the situations you had to deal with at the moment were not much fun, I'm sure, but it's a great read and I'm looking forward to your next one."
—T. Petersen, Puerto Vallarta

"Dammit! I haven't gotten a thing done all afternoon! I can't put D&D down! Thoroughly enjoying the chapter about Jackie Guerrero. You must love her so much. Gotta go and get back to the book."
—P. Thompson, Puerto Vallarta

"D&D brings your emotions to the extreme, first it will make you laugh, then it will make you cry after which you will be trying to figure out how you are going to live in Puerto Vallarta."
—J. Boyd, Mexico City

"Re-read: I'm enjoying the second read even more. I can turn the pages slower and know it just gets better."
—M Shaw, PuertoVallarta

"Gosh. . . I love it. You have a very original style of writing. Have you written any other books I can buy? My husband is a diplomat and I know about the 4 D's. I hear about them every day."
—Miheol, Romanian in Guadalajara

"Your book took me back to those days. . .urns with ashes in the house, etc., You should have included more Canadian assholes."
—N. Johnson, Alberta, Canada, former Canadian Consular Agent

"Ohhmygod" Your book was like I was sitting down with you and having a long, happy visit. What fun reading about my Mom and Dad. THE BOOK is in Cincinatti now and will travel to Phoenix soon. Love the title and the cover! Jack Nicholsan? How did you act so cool? I forget. You're the Queen of Cool. I'd like to buy some more copies to pass around to ardent-to-be fans."
—Dr. L. Moore, Virginia

"I'm glad I found your baby in the grocery store. I love it."
—S. McFarland, Ottawa, Canada

"Of course, you know it is a wonderful book. It takes a very special person to write a book like that. I'm glad you are my friend."

—J. Jones, Ajijic

"I'm loving your book. It is very informative, but witty. Sometimes I laugh out loud; other times I almost cry."

—B. Borzecka, NYC

"You know I must like it since I bought eighteen copies for Christmas gifts."

—J. Galeana, Scottsdale, AZ

"Oh, how that takes me back to the days I lived in PV! Coming in on a cruise ship next week. Please sign me four more copies."

—R. Hulbert, Seattle

PREFACE

Present day Puerto Vallarta is a mature sophisticated city with almost every imaginable product or service available in the world. Air travel to everywhere, luxury cruise liners, limousine service, world-class deep sea fishing; it's all here. Broadband internet, pari-mutuel betting, great health spas, top notch gymnasiums, tennis, eight first class golf courses, PGA tournaments. It has it! Some of the best residential and commercial architects in the world, exceptional restaurants by the dozen, full fledged department stores, and every conceivable class of hotel accommodation.

It was not always thus. The late fifties to early sixties was its infancy. There was little in the way of electricity, no bridge over the Rio Cuale, two or three taxis, and a couple of rudimentary hotels.

Then in 1963, John Huston and crew came to film *The Night of the Iguana*. This event marked the beginning of change in Vallarta which signaled a stirring in its loins. Progress was slow for a while, but by the mid to late sixties, it was showing awkward signs of puberty.

By the late sixties it had two airlines, twelve to fifteen taxis, a tennis court, six to eight hotels, a population of 15,000, and a half dozen acceptable restaurants. As the seventies began, one could discern the obvious: Puerto Vallarta was in full-scale adolescence. Condos began to appear; more beach restaurants and better hotels opened, and in 1974 residential telephone service came to town. Puerto Vallarta was on its way, but not without the stumbling, fumbling, groping of approaching adulthood.

It is to this period of time, the mid seventies to mid nineties, this manuscript is dedicated.

CONTENTS

CHAPTER ONE

Mexican Lovers

Howard and I fell in love with Mexico long before we ever met, and fell in love with each other.

Maude Frickertt, Olga Fernandez and I were fly-girls for American Airlines based in Dallas. The notice went on the bulletin board that screw queduling, that's not a typo; that's what we called it, was looking for girls willing to work the Mexico flights. You either had to speak Spanish, or be willing to take the smallpox vaccine.

I had taken this job with American Airlines to see as much of the United States and Mexico as possible. I thought *equipage* (luggage) was probably a dirty word, but I wanted to see Mexico, so I willingly stuck out my arm for the vaccine.

When I told my family I was going to work as a stewardess and see the world, one of my older brothers scoffed, "Hmmm? Is that what they call them these days? You might as well strap a mattress to your back and put a price tag on your forehead!" That brother adored his baby sister.

Olga was from San Antonio and English was the second language in her home. She was the senior stewardess, which meant I got to do all the dirty work. The first Spanish words I learned were, "What's your name?" and "Buckle up your seat belt." They don't care about names nowadays.

This particular flight was a killer. We made a stop in San Antonio before going on to Mexico City. We always served lunch after leaving San Antonio, and, invariably, we ran into turbulent weather before passing over the Rio Grande River. Even now I can see those hard, little green peas rolling up and down the aisle as coffee or tea splashed about.

The great thing about this flight was that we had seventy-two hours in Mexico City before flying back to Dallas. Of course, we had to sleep a bit, but from the time we hit the Del Prado Hotel, changed clothes and headed for the Nictahai Bar, it was Party Time, Mexico City.

You could walk the streets back then, and the worst that might happen to you would be for a traffic cop to look you up and down, whistle softly between his teeth, and give you that complimentary *"Mamacita!"*

With such a long lay-over we could even fly down to Acapulco for a day on the beach, and still make it back in time for our midnight flight home. We went to bull fights, horse races, and frequented the National Pawn Shop, always looking for a bargain. We ate in fancy restaurants and danced to the violins. You could hire a *mariachi* band to sing a song for you for the equivalent of $.80 cents. Silver bracelets were a dime a dozen and Xochimilco Lake was clean.

We flew with the same crew often. Captain William Platt was a legend. I don't know how he got by with his shenanigans for so long. I guess nobody wanted to blow the whistle on him, because when he was sober, he was a truly likeable guy, and when he was drunk, he went to sleep. Captain Platt was married, but his Significant Other was our Chief Stewardess Supervisor. Neither of these ladies knew about the *Otra Significante* in Mexico City. The rumor was that Platt had won an $80,000 dollar lottery. That was a considerable sum of money in 1956, especially in Mexico, and he kept it there.

Our captain thought he was responsible for his crew the first few hours of our lay-over, and then we were on our own until departure time the next night. He always invited us to dinner at some posh restaurant, but first, we had to visit his *Otra Significante.*

She worked as a B-girl in a ritzy bar in the Zona Rosa district. I didn't know then what a B-girl was, but I was curious why she ordered a shot glass filled with what looked like Coke, while we sipped on beer or tequila. She always sat at our table for two shot glasses of whatever, and then went back to work. Her job was to go sit at some other man's table, so he could buy her another shot glass of Coke.

As long as Olga and I flew that night trip, William Platt never boarded the plane without the help of his First Officer, who piloted the plane back as far as San Antonio. Captain Platt slept all the way.

All three women lost out on the Platt love. He keeled over with a heart attack one day in the airport, before taking his flight out of Dallas. I never met his wife, but I could never figure out what the other two women saw that was so attractive to them.

I finally gained enough seniority to get off the Mexico flight schedule, and went on to visit the big cities of NYC, Washington, D.C., San Francisco, San Diego, Los Angeles, Chicago, Cleveland, and even St. Louis. I went every place I could, but you know the saying, "Once the dust of Mexico has settled on your heart …." That's how my love affair began with Mexico.

I lost track of Olga after Mexico, and we didn't cross paths for another thirty years. We found each other again in Puerto Vallarta, and I thought the years had been very good to her.

In the meantime, Howard was becoming acquainted with another part and another side of Mexico. He's a Texan, and he and his Dallas buddies frequently made the twelve-hour drive to Monterrey. They were a little beyond visiting border towns, and the few extra hours drive was worth the trip, so they declared.

They made life-long friends with a tour guide named Conrado de la Garza. His nickname was Chicken.

A few years rolled by, Howard and I became neighbors, fell in love with each other, and married. Every time we could scrape a few extra pennies together, our car just naturally headed south of the border. Our first trip together to Mexico was to Monterrey. Of course, I had to meet Chicken.

Chicken was driving us around the city one night, and we pulled up at a gaudy, flashing neon sign. Howard began protesting, "Oh, no, Chicken, you wouldn't do this! You wouldn't do this to me!" Chicken got out of the car, holding up his hand, with his thumb and forefinger closed together, the sign for "Just a moment."

Howard was sitting there pounding his knee, and moaning, "Surely, he wouldn't do this!" I had no idea what was going on, but we were someplace where lots of garish red neon lights were flashing.

Soon Chicken reappeared. He opened the car door, jovially clapped Howard on the back and said, "Come on in. I checked it out with the Madam. It's o.k."

That was my introduction to a Mexican brothel. I thought it was hilariously funny, and filed it away to tell my grandchildren about the night their grandmother visited the whore house. I don't think Howard has ever forgiven Chicken for that little sight-seeing trip, but I loved it!

After a few more driving trips throughout Mexico, we decided to set up a ten-year plan to retire. If we had kept focused, we probably would have made it in less than ten years, but we were young, and living a good life in Dallas.

CHAPTER TWO

The First Years

We came to Puerto Vallarta for the first time in August, 1966 and I hated it. The heat was smothering. Air conditioned hotels didn't exist. We played 'swat' with mosquitoes and other unfamiliar flying, biting insects. Our first deep-sea fishing adventure turned out to be a disaster. I don't know if Bruno is still alive or not, but he took us into a school of hungry tuna, the result of which left me looking like a badly abused woman. My fishing chair didn't have a holder for the rod butt, so every time a tuna dived for my hook, it slammed the fishing rod against my inner thighs. With purple bruises on my legs and arms feeling as if they had been pulled from the shoulder sockets, a hold full of flouncing iridescent fish, I begged to be taken back to shore.

The following day we rented a Jeep and felt adventurous enough to go exploring by ourselves. John Huston had filmed *The Night of the Iguana* in Vallarta a couple of years before. Although we had not seen the movie yet, Sue Lyons, Ava Gardner, Elizabeth Taylor and Richard Burton were names being pasted across the pages of newspapers back home. We found the abandoned movie set south of Mismaloya. No doubt I was the nine-hundred-seventy-sixth female tourist to pose under that archway leading from the kitchen to the living room with eyes half closed, trying to look as sexy as Ava Gardner. On that misty, muggy August afternoon, neither of us dreamed that one day we would live in the same neighborhood with Elizabeth and Richard, much less play poker and swap stories with John Huston.

Sunday is bull fight day in Mexico; in big cities, little towns and costal villages. It is about the only event that starts on time, so we were afraid we might miss some of the action when we started looking for a taxi close to four o'clock that afternoon. There were not many taxis in those days and we didn't know that Sunday is usually, or I should say, 'was usually' the one day of the week dedicated to the family. That included taxi drivers. Our problem was solved when a Jeep pulled to the curb alongside us and the dapper driver, with a neatly clipped moustache, asked us in proper English, "Can I give you kids a ride?"

"We're on our way to the bullfight, but there doesn't seem to be any taxis working today", Howard replied.

"Hop in. I'm going that way."

We didn't learn until much later that our chauffeur that day was the main reason Puerto Vallarta became such a popular place with the jet-setters. He was the man who convinced Mr. Huston to film his famous picture here. Name: Guillermo Wulff, Engineer, Architect, Entrepreneur.

We shouldn't have worried about missing the bullfights. The bleachers were still being nailed together when we arrived. The structure seemed rather wobbly as we gingerly climbed up high enough to get a good view, and hopefully, to be out of the way of splattering blood.

After living so many years in Mexico, I've learned to dislike one of its favorite sports. I've learned the poor dumb animal is kept in a pitch-dark stall for forty-eight hours before he is turned loose in the ring to be attacked by the *picador*, the man on horseback who is fully protected from the thrashing, bewildered bull and his sharp horns. The *picador* is armed with a six-inch steel blade mounted on the end of a long pole. His aim is to cause as much trauma to the bull's shoulder muscles as possible. These weakened shoulder muscles lowers the bull's head closer to the ground. making it easier for the *matador* to go in for the kill.

I have to admit there is a certain excitement in the air when the crowd begins to cry out, "*Ole*" as the *matador*, dressed in his 'suit of lights' gracefully dances near the 1,200-or-so-pound beast, teasing him with the sway of his magenta and yellow cape held in his hand. The crowd may be just as easily shouting, "*Ole*" for the bull as the bullfighter. Such was the case the day Engineer Wulff dropped us off at the bullring still under construction.

The *picador* had done his bastardly deed with his sharp lances, the *banderillero* had jabbed barbed sticks into the bloody bull's back, supposedly in order to liven him up for a more realistic fight. Not a chance, poor bull. However, this bull got in a strike of his own to the delight of the crowd and the judge. The over-confident *matador* turned his back on the bull, and walked jauntily toward one side of the viewing stand. The enraged bull lowered his head even lower and charged with all the might he had left. The *matador* heard hooves clamoring behind him, and looked around just as the bull ripped a gash in the back side of his tight-fitting black pants, thereby, exposing his brown *nalgas* to the crowd.

"*Ole! Ole!*" The crowd went wild! People were jumping up and down, whistling, men were tossing their sombreros into the air, women were throwing combs, lipsticks and handkerchiefs into the arena. One woman threw her apron to the bare-bottomed hero who was desperately trying to hide his embarrassment with one hand and manipulate the cape with the other. He managed to get the apron tied around his waist while the bull rested, but the crowd went even crazier when he tried a magnificent veronica, pivoting around to shake the cape in front of the bull's eyes, daring him to come closer. He had tied the apron around his waist, but upside down. The part which is supposed to go around the neck made a perfect frame for the bull's art work.

While dancing on Los Muertos Beach in La Palapa Restaurant, my foot became bosom buddies with an iron table leg. I don't know if I broke it or not, but it swelled up to about the size of a watermelon, and turned a deep purple. A beach vender wanted to put leeches on it to suck the blood out! Gaud! I couldn't wait to go home.

About a year and a half passed before we decided to come back and see if Puerto Vallarta really was as bad as we remembered. We spent Christmas here that year and the rest becomes history.

We didn't make the permanent move until 1973, but we set up temporary housekeeping in one of Freddy Romero's bungalows in Las Campanas, behind the downtown cathedral. As a matter of fact, the church bells would just about knock us off the terrace in the afternoons. We rented Casa Rebeca, named after Freddy's baby daughter.

We kept that place for five years, coming down as often as we could, and loaning it out to our friends when we couldn't come. One year we invited Howard's work companions and their spouses down for a week-long party. They all stayed in what was the El Dorado Hotel. Casa Rebeca was the official meeting place.

By July 1973 we had sold our home in Dallas, had one of those popular garden sales, and stored a few pieces of furniture, which we couldn't part with, in friends' homes. We packed several bulging suitcases into a brand new orange Datsun station wagon, and drove out of town to the jeers of friends, every one of them fully expecting us to come wagging our tails back home within six months.

We've been back many times in the past thirty-odd years, but home is definitely where the heart is. That's Mexico.

We didn't have much money, but things didn't cost much either. We were the youngest kids on the block and new blood in town. Retirement life was an active party life.

Elizabeth Taylor and Richard Burton had just bought Casa Kimberly. The truth is that Elizabeth bought a house on the upper side of Zaragoza Street in a neighborhood that is still called Gringo Gulch, due to so many gringos settling in that area. Richard surprised Liz by buying a house on the opposite side of the street. Then they built a bridge over the street, connecting the two houses, and painted it pink. Little known to many people, they also built an escape door from the swimming pool area on Richard's side into Phil and Jane Ober's house, which faced Cuauhtemoc Street, one street below Zaragoza. When the reporters were waiting for them to come out the front door on Zaragoza, they sneaked through the Ober house and were off down Cuauhtemoc, leaving the press with their notepads and cameras in hand.

After enjoying visits to Casa Rebecca for five years, we didn't make it through the first rainy season. As with so many of the houses Romero built in the Gulch, you had to go outside to get to the bath and bedrooms. Along about mid-August of that first year, what few walls we had were turning green. The cobblestone walkways throughout the maze of bungalows were dangerously slippery with mold. Shoes turned green, clothes never really got dry; even the leather equipale chairs and tables were greening. It was the average hot, humid, Puerto Vallarta summer.

One day while Howard was out shopping, one of those torrential downpours came. If you've ever been here in the summer, you know what I mean. The sky opens and the streets become rivers, some even white-capping.

The wind was blowing from all directions. Curtains of water blew in tossing chairs, tables, and potted ferns topsy turvy. I was furious that my playhouse was being messed up! I picked up every piece of furniture I could handle, and threw it over the balcony. The stove and refrigerator were old and rusty, and I wanted to buy new ones anyway, but they were too heavy for me, or they would have gone over with the furniture.

At last the sky closed a bit. The river became a street again and Howard made his way into the compound stepping over chairs, tables, and broken bits of pottery and glass. He found me sitting on top of the stove. "I want to move someplace else," I sobbed.

In 1969, on one of our vacations to Puerto Vallarta, we had made friends with two other married couples. Bill and Sue Glover were from Lima, Ohio. Bill was in the dry cleaning business. Helen and Don Goldsmith were from Connecticut. Don was a successful realtor and Helen owned a very up-scale dress shop.

The six of us reserved umbrellas and chairs at El Dorado Beach on a daily basis. That was a sign you were a Regular. I believe the Goldsmiths still have their special umbrella spot.

We met Chico Lopez. Chico was married to a very pregnant Franceska, an American from Wisconsin. Chico had this grandiose idea of building three condominiums and a small apartment on a piece of land he owned up on the hillside overlooking the bay.

He was a smooth talker. He would have been a good time-share salesman. All of us fell for his line and his idea like a sack of bricks. Chico and Franceska were to have the ground floor apartment. The Goldsmiths and Glovers were to share the next level, with a one bedroom apartment each. We planned to live there full-time, whereas the other couples would be winter residents only. We chose the penthouse.

Chico needed front money to get started. Each couple advanced him one year's rent. I tell you, things were cheap back then. Our penthouse rent cost us $2,500 dollars for the year.

Sue, Helen and I had fabulous decorating ideas. Helen could afford nicer furniture than Sue and I. Sue picked out rustic hand-made furniture. She planned to have a totally blue and white house. I hoped to fill our empty spaces with plants and a few leather chairs.

Franceska and Chico's baby boy arrived. Chico was on the construction site every day. A man called Precious Ramon was his head worker with several peon helpers mixing, toting, plastering, and tiling. The first floor apartment was shaping up nicely.

One afternoon Franceska left the baby with the *niñera*, the baby sitter, and took a walk up the hill to the new condo building. To her surprise, and Chico's also, she found two brown bodies busily grunting, pumping, and rutting on the newly laid tile floor.

Her packing was done quickly. I visited with her the day before the movers were due to arrive. As I watched her gently wrap a dime store salt shaker in several layers of newspaper, I asked her, "Why,

Kika, why?" She grimly told me, "I'm taking everything I ever put into this marriage. I'm taking his son, whom he'll never see again; I'm not leaving anything here except Chico Lopez."

"But why, Kika? Why did you ever marry him in the first place?" I wondered.

"Brown fever," she answered. "All of us gringas get it at one time or the other. Age old question. Age old answer. I thought I could change him."

With Kika's guiding hand gone, construction slowed, and then came to a stop for a few years.

Sue was the first one who thought of the gambit to get some of our advance money back from Chico. He was the chef at a well-known restaurant on Los Muertos Beach, which his sister, Rosalina, owned. Sue and Bill invited a group of friends to lunch at the restaurant and signed the tab, leaving a generous tip for the waiters.

They entertained and signed, entertained and signed, and encouraged us to do the same. We did. After all, we were Regulars on the beach. We were well known and lots of folks ran open tabs.

Saturday was Collection Day. One day, little brother, Lencho Lopez, was sent out to collect from the clients. He arrived at the Glovers' condo first. Sue sent him packing, telling him, "Chico owes me money. This is my way of collecting." She forewarned us with a phone call before Lencho could knock on our door. I told the boy, "Look, son, Chico owes me money. We'll pay this bill when he pays us. Be on your way!"

In less than twenty minutes, the kid was back at our door with a message: "My sister Rosalina says that Chico may owe you money, but this is what you owe her," as he handed us a stack of bills we had signed.

We paid, of course, but the game didn't stop there. That grunting, pumping, rutting floor was re-financed by some other sucker, and it became what was the kitchen of Sr. Lopez' Restaurant. I only stiffed him one time in the restaurant on the hillside.

He went on to open Lopez' Paradise Restaurant, south of town where two dangerous rivers meet. It was a beautiful spot, but numerous lives were lost when the rivers flash-flooded and caught the swimmers unaware. I always wanted to put up a cross along the bank for every person who drowned there, but Chico wouldn't even allow me to put up a cautioning sign.

The last time we collected from him was at this Paradise. Our style had become routine. We wrote a nice note of gratitude on the back of the bill, left a handsome tip for the waiter, and got up from our table to leave.

Chico was behind the grill, sweating, fuming, and furious as we walked by. I sweetly smiled, lowered my head and innocently looked into his eyes. I knew then that we would never do this again. His debt was cancelled.

I instantly recalled a story he had told us when we first met. He had worked as a waiter at Hotel Posada Vallarta when it opened. Some rather obnoxious guests had pestered him for several days.

One day those guests wanted a box lunch prepared for them to take out on a fishing boat. Chico prepared it. He laughed as he told how he put several drops of syrup of ipecac in the mayo he spread on the ham sandwiches. He filled their thermos with tap water.

The hotel guests didn't enjoy their fishing trip, and I was afraid we wouldn't enjoy our next meal with Chico.

Not many days passed after my stove-top-roosting episode before Sue Glover appeared at Casa Rebeca. She was very excited that she had just bought a one-bedroom condo on Piño Suarez Street, two blocks from Los Muertos Beach. She told us there were two other condos for sale in the same building. We had to take a look.

We looked. We liked what we saw, and bought. Sue and I thought we should share the good news with the Goldsmiths.

Helen flew in from New York, wearing an absolutely stunning ultra-suede pant suit. To Puerto Vallarta? In September?

She bought the remaining condo, and we all started remodeling. I don't know how we met Cruz Ornelas. Maybe our new neighbors, Ginny and Irv Serlin told us about him. Cruz became our life-long contractor friend.

He installed a circular stairway from one end of our terrace up to our next door neighbor's open flat roof. We signed a contract with the neighbor and paid him "$1.00 dollar and other good and valuable considerations" in exchange for air space. There we built our laundry room.

Almost all buildings down here have water tanks on the roof tops. You can buy or build a cement wash basin with a scrub board. The scrub board is made of cement, and it is corrugated or ribbed like an old fashioned metal scrub board. There's a drain hole at the bottom of this contraption. Attached to the scrub board is a small basin fixed with a tap allowing it to be filled from the big tank on the roof. These laundry areas are called *pilas*.

We rigged up a sort of canvas awning to cover the area, and to give some protection from the sun for the wash lady. We strung lines across the roof top and our clothes dried in no time, flapping in the breeze.

One day while this roof top work was going on, Cruz walked in with a dead baby pig in his arms. He'd been doing his farm chores earlier that morning, and this piglet kept getting in his way. In frustration, and with too much gusto, he picked up an ear of corn, and hit the pig smack dab in the middle of his head. Killed it on the spot.

Cruz knew about butchering hogs. He had worked in a meat market, called a *carneceria*, at one time. I had seen this done on my own farm back home, and I knew the first thing women did was put on water to boil.

We decided the butchering should take place in Sue's garden downstairs. Cruz had a rope and pulley in his truck, and he hung the pig from a palm tree. Sue and I boiled water in galvanized mop buckets. Cruz would do the scraping, gutting and butchering. Howard and Bill had an immediate need to visit the liquor store. After all, we were planning a roast suckling pig dinner, and we needed the proper wine to go along with it.

Sue was an outstanding cook. We nicknamed each other Sara Lee I and Sara Lee II. I was II. We insisted that Cruz bring his wife, Catalina, to dinner that night. That pig cemented a friendship with the Ornelas family that is still strong.

Every day was party day. It was not unusual to go to three parties in one day.

We were young vital, healthy, eager folks back then. The neighborhood baker woke us up at 5:00 a.m. with the delicious aroma of fresh baked bread. We were on the tennis court or swimming in the ocean by 7:00 a.m. Nine o'clock usually found us downtown running errand. I don't remember what sort of errands we ran, but we thought they were important. Kept us on track, you see.

By 10:30 a.m. it was time to get dressed for the first social event of the day. Eleven o'clock was a good hour for the first Bloody Mary, followed by a sumptuous brunch, and then it was time to go home and rest before the 2:00 p.m. luncheon.

This was truly a strenuous lifestyle, but somebody had to keep up the image of the jet setters in Puerto Vallarta, and we were willing volunteers. The evening get-togethers were much easier. We had eaten well all day, played a little bridge or poker if there was time, soaked up some sun on the beach or on our terraces, and maybe even read a book.

None of us had cablevision or Direct T.V. A few of us had short-wave radios, and strangely enough, we all longed for news from home. Phil Ober had the strongest radio, and he kept us up to date on what was going on in the world.

Visiting friends from El Norte used to ask me, "But what in the world do you do all day?"

I always answered, "I don't know. I get up in the morning with nothing to do; I go to bed at night and I haven't gotten half of it done."

One day, Sue and I decided we were turning as green as our summer walls. We thought we might teach English, so we went to see Rosa Baumgarten.

Rosa was the wife of Don Jose, the mayor of Puerto Vallarta. That made her president of IMPI, Instituto Mexicano for the Protection of the Infantiles. Rosa's office was big, black leather, snap-lock purse, which sat open on her ample lap when she was conducting one of her meetings in somebody's home.

I loved that purse. One of my sisters had one just like it. She kept her marriage license in it, along with all her children's birth certificates, measles, smallpox, typhoid, and whooping cough vaccination records. Rosa kept scraps of paper with handwritten notes in hers. Nobody knows what her filing system was, but she could rummage around in that black bag and come up with the number of kids in Desmoronada going to school in the thatched roof shack who needed shoes.

Desmoronada was just another one of the poorer outlying neighborhoods. It wasn't until many years later that the foreign colony became involved in community projects and began building schools, playgrounds, and child-care centers around town.

Rosa was thrilled with the idea that the two gringas wanted to teach English. She had teachers for classes in sewing, cake decorating, and hair cutting, but English classes would be something they didn't even have in the big cities.

For about two years we taught in the school up the river, in a neighborhood called El Remance. We learned quickly that the kids' attention span was about twenty minutes, if that long.

Teachers are almost revered in Mexico, unlike in the United States, and some other parts of the world. There is even a national holiday, May 15, which is called Teachers Day. Of course, there is no school that day, but there are parties, feasts, and drunken brawls, all in honor of The Teacher.

One of my friends taught school in the mountains above Puerto Vallarta for fifty-five years. Her name is Rosario Cibrian de Leon, but she is known as La Maestra, The Teacher. Rosario visits family in the United States frequently. She says she runs into some of her former students every time she goes to Oakland, San Diego, or anywhere in the San Bernardino Valley area. She can always count on hearing, "Hola, Maestra!" whenever she goes out.

Does that tell you anything about our closed border policy?

Our next mayor was Eugenio Torres, whose charismatic wife; Martha Andalon de Torres became the president of IMPI. This was the year the federal government decided to expand this organization and change the name to DIF, Development of the Integral Family. Martha told us she did a lot of "pillow talking" to get a run-down building, donated by the city for a DIF office.

I think that must have been about the time the federal government decided to pay a salary to the state governors' and city mayors' wives for the very important roles they play in their community.

Not only did Martha have an office with a bonafide desk; she had an assistant, her loyal friend, Mari Francis Inez de Baños. They both had secretaries. The secretaries had manual typewriters. No computers yet.

Somebody donated an old beat-up van, which they had painted white with big red letters on the side, DIF. Tacho was their driver. His teeth and gums would have given nightmares to dentists, and he loved to smile.

Two rooms in the DIF building were set aside for Sue and me as English classrooms. We taught for an hour twice a week. Martha's pillow-talking didn't provide blackboards for us. We bought those ourselves.

About this time of our teaching career, Sue went back to Ohio to try to get Bill elected as the County Sheriff. Howard and I decided to enroll in the Instituto in San Miguel de Allende, Guanajuato for advanced Spanish language classes. While we were there, I was asked to teach English in night classes. This gave me an idea.

When we came home from San Miguel, I opened my own language school. I hired a Mexican Baptist minister to teach Spanish. There aren't many of those, you know. I taught three groups of English students, but I also continued with the English classes in DIF.

There was a young girl in one of the DIF classes who was better than any of the other students. She was about thirteen years old and looked about nine. We called her Jackie.

We were still playing tennis. A new tennis club was under construction, and we were eagerly waiting for it to open since we heard it would have a swimming pool, locker rooms and a good restaurant. This sounded good because we could shower after our sweaty tennis matches, have a light lunch and play bridge the rest of the afternoon, before the cocktail party hour. Man, oh, man, we had a tough life. Nobody worked, but we sure kept busy.

While the new club was being built, we kept our 7:30 morning reservation at the only other public court in town. I believe the John Newcomb courts were probably laid over the spot where we played.

It was old. The broken-surface had grass growing through the cracks, the net was badly mended, but the court was swept clean daily by an old man named Fernando Guerrero.

Everybody in town knew Don Fernando. After his chore of clearing the tennis court every morning, he started out on his rounds at his main job. He sold lottery tickets, and the story was that he had sold some big winners in Puerto Vallarta. Big winners show their appreciation just like they do in Las Vegas.

Don Fer worked hard all day. He called on his customers in City Hall, the Pemex gas station, the airport, the post office, and the newspaper offices. He had steady customers all over town plus the ones he picked up on the streets. By three o'clock in the afternoon, he had worked himself down to El Dorado Restaurant on Los Muertos Beach and had also worked up a colossal thirst. How he got to his home, I don't know. He may have had a Rolls-Royce parked around the corner, but I don't think so.

One morning Howard was warming up with a few balls over the net as Don Fer was busy sweeping the last bit of sand from the court. He and I got into a conversation about his children. He told me they had all sneaked across the border into the United States and gotten married. He only had one little girl left at home, but he figured she would leave him also as soon as she finished what we would call Junior High School or Middle School.

I asked Don Fer how old his daughter was. "*Va cumplir trece.*" She's going to be thirteen.

"And what's her name?" I asked.

"Jacqueline."

"That's Jackie Guerrero," I thought.

"Don Fernando, I think I know your little girl. She is in one of my DIF English classes."

"*Asi es,*" he agreed, with a big smile that showed a missing tooth or two. "That's right."

"Listen," I told him. "Let's make a deal. You let Jackie study with me in private classes for three months, and one of these days I'll give you a bilingual secretary. She'll never leave you." And that is the way it happened.

By now we had sold our condo on Piño Suarez Street. The Glovers had split after Bill failed to win the County Sheriff's seat. Sue had sold her condo and moved to Chicago. We had moved into Gringo Gulch. The Goldsmiths had sold their condo and bought another at the new El Dorado Condominium complex.

Liz and Richard had split, but she still owned Casa Kimberly. Richard had married Susan Hunt and their house, BurSu, was around the corner from us. We could stand on our terrace of Casa Capricornio, and look down on the famous pink bridge of Casa Kimberly, and look over to the right and see the rooftop of Casa BurSu.

Mind you, I'm not name-dropping. I never met Richard Burton, and as close as I ever came to meeting Liz Taylor was when she left a message on my answering machine one day. Her secretary, who always traveled with her, had managed to lose her tourist card.

Doctor Jose Romo got to know her intimately on one of her visits. She thought she might be having a heart attack. He made a house call. I've heard that later he had his stethoscope dipped in liquid gold, and that it hangs on a wall in his secret Trophy Room.

Besides attending her regular school classes, Jackie was working part-time at Ric's jewelry store. She was studying accounting and working diligently on her English. She even set up her own English classes out in El Pitillal, one of our suburbs. Lest I bore you with Jackie, she is now working on her twenty-five year lapel pin at the American Consular Agency in Puerto Vallarta. .

CHAPTER THREE

Dirty Poker, Movers, Shakers & Wannabees

Between tennis playing, partying and teaching English, we participated in a floating poker game. Actually, there were two games in town. Sue Glover and I were allowed in The Sunday Game, which was a super- friendly game with low stakes, and we took turns hosting the game in our homes and providing a simple lunch.

Dr. Brooks Pringle, Ken Hosfield, Dan Danley, Frank Walker, Sue, Howard and I made up the table. I think this must have been when I learned to tell when people were lying … at least some of the time. Nowadays I see professional poker players wearing sunglasses, long billed caps pulled low over their foreheads and even chewing on unlit cigarettes or cigars. We used none of those props; just never thought about it I guess.

Brooks had the easiest 'tell' of all. He was a short, stockily-built balding man with beady blue eyes, and he wore hearing aids in both ears. He could never quite get his ante into the middle of the table, but on the occasions he won, which were frequent, he could certainly manage to lean in and rake the chips to his side of the table. We knew Brooks thought he had a winning hand when he sat up straighter, darted those beady eyes around the cards on the table and started whistling under his breath. Watch out! He's on the path again!

Ken faked total indifference. He appeared to be more interested in what was happening outside rather than the cards falling on the table or the others' bets.

Frank was one of our token artists back in the late seventies. In fact, Sue and I, among others, took art lessons from him. We didn't use paints or brushes. The class shared a big box of pastel chalks, but each of us brought our own t-squares to class. I'm not joshing! There was no individual spontaneity encouraged. We all drew the same still-life and we measured the distance between the apple and the banana, not with the upheld thumb, but with our t-squares. Frank's complexion tended to be on the ruddy side, possibly alcohol induced. When he was dealt a good hand, all color drained from his face. His black, slicked-backed hair and his dark eyes stood out against the paleness of his skin. Look out! Frank is gonna bet!

Sue perspired a little heavier, Dan's fingers trembled, and two pairs with a possibility of a full house had me dropping cards and knocking water glasses over; in other words, acting extremely nonchalant.

Most of the Sunday Game players were not allowed in the Big Boys Game, which was also a floater. These were the heavy hitters, heavy betters, and although they were friendly guys, they had bigger fish to fry than a bunch of Sunday kindergarteners.

The Big Boys were Phil Ober, John Huston, William (aka) Billy Joe Reed, Paul Bancroft, Ernesto Ramirez, Perry Hester, Thomas Carpentino, and sometimes Miguel Escontria and Howard. Big hitters like the fat pig, Dr. Eufracio Contreras and one of the biggest Wannabes I ever met, Kirby Finnegan, didn't come along until most of the core group was well on their way to their graves as Billy Joe strummed his guitar and sang, "Oh, Danny Boy, me heart is calling..."

Once a week this group floated from houses to condos to tiny apartments, even back rooms of restaurants, until they finally found a permanent home at Suzy Long's pad in Gringo Gulch along the Rio Cuale.

Suzy had a story of her own to tell and it is our loss she never wrote it before taking her leave of this world. Suzy started her marrying life when she was a young woman and continued it well into her menopausal years. Once she told me, "My first husband had sexier nightgowns than I did, and his lipstick was a prettier shade of pink than mine." However, they performed their marital obligations, at least twice, to the delight of her in-laws. One result of this nuptial uniting is now living in Leavenworth, guest of the U. S. Government, and the other is also a guest of the U.S. Government in Washington, D.C. She suffers from BPD---Borderline Personality Disorder. The truth is: many of us may have BPD, but we are not distinguished guests of the U.S. Government.

While the Big Boys were still touring the neighborhood and before they found their permanent home with Suzy, one game took place south of town in a high rise, beach front condominium. Ernesto Ramirez --- one of the biggest hitters and the owner of the largest and most successful restaurant in town, Las Margaritas --- never left his bed without a .45 automatic stashed in his tooled leather bag which he carried over his shoulder.

The game played throughout the hot afternoon with the sun streaming through the window facing the ocean. The men took off their shirts, and played as sweat poured from their brows and over their torsos. The stakes were high and some lost more than they could afford, while others lined their pockets for the next week's game.

This group had a time limit and usually ended the game around 5 o'clock in the afternoon. This day was different and those who had won a bit of change anticipated an extension of the game. Howard was eager to continue and chimed in, "Count me in. I'm staying."

Ernesto sauntered over to Howard and under his breath said, "Go on home, Howard. I like you, but this is not a good place for you now. If that bastard, Perry Hester, palms one more card, I'll put a bullet through his head. I don't want you or any other gringos involved."

I doubt that Ernesto had anything to do with it, but the rumor later floated through the poker community that Hester's body was found by deep-sea divers in Acapulco. He still had his shoes on, but they were filed with some type of building substance; cement, I think it is called.

I guess this is as good a place as any to admit I've changed some of my characters names. Trust me, they existed, and it is not their innocence I'm worried about. My editors are too busy with problems of their own to bring me egg sandwiches.

Seven weeks after Howard started playing with the Big Boys his turn came to host the game. I had known this time would come and I wondered how I would handle it. I had heard about what Phil Ober's always-tipsy cook, Juana, served for lunch. Naturally, John Huston had his accomplished chef, Archie. We had enjoyed many dinners at Paul Bancroft's house, skillfully prepared by his and Kitty's loyal Francesca. Our gun-toting friend, Ernesto, being a restaurateur, could serve anything off his extensive menu. I knew about Bea Escontria's Swiss-American-Mexican background, and how she mixed those cultures' cuisines into her own kitchen.

Sylvia Reed has exhibited her gourmet culinary talents on many occasions. Her husband, Billy Joe, either lies a lot or forgets the stories he told in the past. These days he says the reason he married Sylvia is because she walked up into the jungle in Mismaloya, where he was living in his trailer, and prepared him the most succulent *coq au vin* he had ever tasted. Some thirty years ago, he told me a different story about why he married her. Granted, she definitely has her culinary skills, but if you want to know what I think is the truth, she was the first woman he had ever met who could look right into his soul, and see what the U.S. Government didn't see. Alas. Weep forevermore, CIA and NSA. Yeah, among many other things, Billy Joe was an ex-spook.

It came our time to, literally, step up to the plate and fill it. Instead of high-rise condominium or a hacienda with a sweeping veranda overlooking the ocean, we lived in a scant nine-hundred-square-foot, third-floor walkup apartment. We had a table that served four comfortably, but could not accommodate seven burly men. Howard's carpenter friend came to the rescue and made an extra-large table top to set on the top of our little table. We had inherited nice dishes with the purchase of this tiny pad in the sky, so that was not my concern.

It was customary for the food preparer to be far in the background; I might add, so far into the background he/she could not be seen until the moment of serving the meal. I didn't have a kitchen helper or a hiding place in our small apartment, so I did as much advance preparation as possible and hid out in our neighbor's garden until the Appointed Hour of Serving.

Now you tell me, what is a girl from Mississippi … especially one so young as I … going to prepare and serve to a famous Hollywood film director, a movie star, a prominent international author and a rich San Francisco socialite, whose favorite pastime was trying to beat John Huston at backgammon?

I trembled as I walked back into the apartment to put the finishing touches on what I would serve to Howard's poker buddies. I was introduced to John, the only one of the group whom I had not met: grey hair that needed cutting, grey beard that needed trimming, the tall gangly man whose arms seemed to reach below his knees stood and began a conversation, which lasted over twenty years, "It is a pleasure to meet you, my dear".

My day was a smashing success when the *caballeros* filed past the buffet I had set out for them: veal birds, mashed potatoes, gravy, beets set on a bed of lettuce, green beans and pickled *papaya*. When John Huston came to table, he exclaimed, "Oh, how I love color in a dinner!"

That comment has resounded in our house all these years. Whenever I happen to fix a pretty table, Howard always compliments me by saying, "John would approve of this."

Thomas Carpentino … according to him … prepared excellent Italian food. I cannot tell you if that is true or not because I never was at his table. I took him an egg sandwich while he was in jail for not paying his rent. I collected his bail bond from his poker-playing buddies and I read and re-read the scathing letter he wrote to the State Department accusing me of not helping him in his time of trouble.

We ran into Thomas in Queretaro many years after the poker game had folded. As a matter of fact, we stayed in Queretaro several weeks and we kept bumping into Thomas on the streets. Every time we saw him, he said, "We must get together for dinner."

We decided to pre-empt him and invited him to brunch in a restaurant. Once again, he regaled us with his cooking skills and said he cooked at a local Italian restaurant from time to time to entertain his friends. All of sudden, he stopped his diatribe in mid sentence and cried out, "Oh, my God! I almost invited you for dinner! Can you imagine that?" We couldn't.

If a mouse could relate the tales he heard at these poker games, he would be the biggest rat in town. The best one I ever heard is, actually, Howard's recount to me, which I will share with you:

"It was my turn to deal. We played the game according to Hoyle, in other words, the cards called themselves; the player only turned the cards over and bet on them.

The game was seven-card stud. Four or five players were hanging on waiting for the fifth card to be dealt. Paul Bancroft put in a strong bet and all folded except John. John called Paul's bet and the sixth card was dealt. Paul put in another big bet and John called.

John's up card was a king of diamonds. Paul stuck with his heavy betting, and after glancing at his up card, John called him again. The last card was dealt down. Paul pushed all of his chips into the center of the table; so did John. Paul turned over aces full with sevens. John glanced at Paul's hand, never looking at his own last down card, picked up all his cards and tossing them into the center of the table grumbling, "All I have is a flush."

There on the table were the six, nine, ten, jack, queen and king of diamonds. I was so astonished, I yelled, 'But John, it's a straight flush!'

John knew he had made his flush on the sixth card and never bothered looking at his seventh down card, which was the *queen of diamonds*.

Needless to say, I never heard the last of that from my good friend Paul. He never passed up the opportunity to mimic me, "But John, it's a straight flush!"

How I miss those guys! There is only me and Billy Joe left to swap tall tales.

CHAPTER FOUR

Early Days In The Consular Agency

Party days were coming to an end. Phil and Jane Ober had entertained our foreign community with tales of their travels on cargo ships, their Hollywood days, the early construction days of Casa Juanita built by the town's well-known Architect Guillermo Wulff and his even better known tricks of the trade. The Obers loved Memo Wulff.

Phil's lung x-ray was not as pretty as the doctor thought it should be. He flew to Los Angeles for the second opinion and returned to Puerto Vallarta to put things in order.

Forever the great gentleman, *El Gran Caballero,* he talked to Howard before he talked to me. We were in Casa Juanita, walking up into the entertainment area from the garden entry, when Phil turned to Howard and asked, "Do I have your permission to train Jenny to take over this work when I leave?"

Neither of us knew what we were getting ourselves into when Howard said, "Why, sure, Phil."

We didn't know how much time we had to learn the ropes and the loops in those ropes. I used to say to him, "Aiiiiiii, yaiiii, yaiii, Phil! How am I ever going to do this?" His motto was a strong one. He always answered, "The best you can, girl. Do the best you can."

CHAPTER FIVE

Foreign Affairs Manuals

Foreign Affairs Manuals were called FAM's, and I believe there might have been twelve volumes which pertained to consular services in foreign countries. They were at least five inches thick and bound in big black three-ringed binders. The print was so fine I could never read it these days, but no procedure was left untouched.

There was an explicit word-for-word description of how you had to make out an estate inventory when somebody died in your consular district. If the deceased left twelve pairs of socks, you listed that item:

```
12 pair of socks
1 brown, 8 white, 2 black, 1 green w/hole in toe    $ 6.00
Cash                                                $25.00
1 ring, yellow-colored metal w/clear stone          N/A
```

I appreciated the fact that we never called a diamond a diamond; a gold ring a gold ring, nor put a value on these items, but we could sure say a worn-out pair of dirty socks probably would bring $.50 in a Flea Market.

These Estate Inventories Forms were supposed to be signed by the person making the inventory and a reliable, knowledgeable witness.

Caramba! How could you come up with a reliable, knowledgeable witness when you weren't even sure what you were doing yourself?

During the time I was working, there were thirty-two consular agents scattered around the world. There were more assigned to Mexico than any other country. Eighteen of us, from different parts of the world, were invited to Washington, D.C. for a week-long training class sometime after we had been working for a few years.

We learned more about the famous FAM's, and one old-timer advised us not to worry too much about them. He told us the State Department really had four categories in mind, which consular agents should be mostly concerned with. He called them The Four D's.

1. Death
2. Detention
3. Destitute
4. Disappearance

He never told us about Dirty Old Men, Demented, Derelicts, and most especially, never told us about the Derogatory Abuse we would face.

Not intentionally, but knowingly, I broke every rule written in those FAM's. In the mid-80's I never had the time to consult with 109.34 Section XII of 3 FAM, Consular Affairs. Some folks have called it the School of Hard Knocks. Others said it was Flying by the Seat of Your Pants. I don't know. I just got the job done the best way I could. That's what I did. Now, come take a walk with me through some of the shadier, seamier sides of diplomacy abroad. There are some sunny spots on the street also. Enjoy.

CHAPTER SIX

Destitutes

Meaning: Without resources. No money, no place to sleep, no food to eat, and sometimes no clean clothes either. No family back home, no friends who can help out. Nobody, except our US Government. Thank God, we have a government which provides its' citizens a way out of the mess they usually have gotten themselves into in a foreign country.

Phil Ober was still alive when I met my first Destitute. He and Jane were off on one of their fifty-two-day cargo ship cruises, and he had left me in charge.

On Cuauhtemoc Street, in about the 400 block, there is a wooden post sticking up out of the sidewalk. It looks old and worn enough that it might have been a hitching post. I never learned why it was there, but it marked the end of the row of houses, which had been built along the Cuale River in Gringo Gulch, and there sat my first encounter with a Destitute.

As Howard and I were driving down the street, I saw an old man, greasy, graying yellow hair, which hung below his ears, dressed about like the bums I had seen in the Bowery, leaning on that wooden post, and I cried out, "Stop, stop the car, Howie! There's one! There's a destitute American! He needs me! Stop the car!"

"Are you totally out of your mind, or what?" Howard asked.

We stopped. I got out of the car, approached the old man, and questioned him, "You look like an American. I'm an assistant to Phil Ober. He represents the United States of America in this town. You look as if you could use a friend. Can I help?"

Phineas T. Booker said to me, "I been looking fer ya. They told me at the hotel you wuz over here somewheres."

Howard parked the car and we walked back to our house. Phineas' story was like so many I later heard.

"I met a friend in a bar, and we got to talking about books. I told him I had some books back at the hotel I'd give him. He come back with me, and while I wuz in the bathroom taking a shaur, he stole my billfold and my blood pressure medicine."

"What kind of blood pressure medicine are you taking?" I asked.

"Well, Miz Gills, I take a white pill in the morning fer my low blood pressure and I take a blue pill at night fer my high blood pressure."

I'm not a nurse, but I had learned how to take blood pressure readings. My nephew, The Doctor, had provided us with a Physicians Desk Reference, medical dictionary, an old sphygmomanometer, cuff, and stethoscope when we had moved here. I pulled this paraphernalia out from my bottom desk drawer and told Phineas, "Roll up your sleeve."

He was reading 190/120.

Howard had recently been prescribed medication for his high blood pressure, so I called Dr. Paul de Silva.

"What do you think, Paul? Would it be safe to give him one of Howard's pills?"

"Can't hurt him. Give it a try," he advised.

That's how I became Miz Doctor Gills.

When I told Phineas that Dr. de Silva had said that it would be alright for him to take one of Howard's pills to lower his blood pressure, he asked me, "Could I have a drank?"

"Sure, Phineas, just hold this pill while I get you a glass of water."

"I'll take vodka iffen you got some."

Phineas washed his blue pill down with vodka while I filled out a form which we called a Repatriation Loan. Travel was inexpensive in those days. Bus fare to Guadalajara was approximately $3.50 US, taxi fare from the bus station to the Consulate General was about $2.50, so a ten-dollar bill would buy him something to eat and he would be on his way for help.

I don't know what the State Department does in other parts of the world, but in Mexico and Canada the FAM directed us to repatriate to the nearest border point in the most economic way. From Puerto Vallarta, that meant to Guadalajara by bus, then on to Laredo by bus. It didn't make any difference that you lived in California. If you wanted to go home, the FAM said you went through Texas.

Phineas signed the Repatriation Loan and Promise-to-Pay forms, took his peso equivalent of $10.00, and I thought he was on his way back to his home in Arizona, after stopping at the Consulate General for a refill on his travel money.

I doubt Phineas ever left town because he was back at our door in a few days. Remember that I was new at this. I was merely covering for Phil while he and Jane were cruising in South America.

"Phineas!" I cried, "You've come to pay me back, haven't you?"

"You won't believe this, Miz Doctor Gills, but I got nuthin in my pocket 'cept my comb. Somebody on the bus stole my cab money and I couldn't even get to the Consulate, so I hitched a ride back here to Porto Valarty."

I hadn't learned all the tricks yet, but I was catching on.

"There's no more money, but I'll fix you a sandwich, and you can go on your way. Try hitchhiking back to the border this time," I told him.

"That's mighty nice of ya, Miz Doctor Gills. Could I have a drank with my sandwich?"

"You sure can, but no vodka this time. Water or milk?" I asked.

"I'll jez take the sandwich and be on my way," he muttered as he walked out the door.

I thought that was the end of my Destitute American Booker, but some of our friends told us they had seen him stopping other Americans on the street asking for hand-outs. Weeks passed and I heard nothing more about him. Then one night I received a call from the Vallarta Hospital about two American male patients.

I went to the hospital, and there was Phineas and another man whose name I never even bothered to ask. They had been in the hospital for two nights feigning great pain to the doctors. Strangely enough, this pain didn't affect their appetite. They were getting three squares a day plus a place to sleep. They didn't have a clue of what danger they were in until I explained to them that jail food was not very good, and the cots had no mattresses. They were gone by morning, and I never heard from Phineas T. Booker again.

My next encounter with a destitute American traveler was swift and almost painless. After Phineas, I thought I could handle anything.

A young man came to the office one afternoon with the tale that he had lost his tourist card and billfold. He still had his return airline ticket, but he needed taxi fare, airport departure tax, and a replacement for his tourist card. He offered me a gold bracelet. He asked for a loan of $50.00 dollars on the bracelet, promising to send me a check as soon as he got home. I bit. I figured I couldn't lose. The bracelet was probably worth at least $200.00 dollars. If he didn't send the check, then I would have a nice gold bracelet for $50.00 dollars. We made our exchange and he went on his way.

Remember that Jackie had worked part-time in a jewelry store before becoming a consular assistant. I could hardly wait for her to arrive at work the following morning. As soon as she walked in the door, I dangled the bracelet in front of her, and quipped, "Look what I've got! How much do you think this is worth?"

She took the bracelet from me, held it in her hand, and weighed it up and down. "How much did you pay for it, Jenny?"

"Fifty dollars!" I proudly declared.

She raised her eyebrows, shrugged her shoulders, and looked at me sadly, "You've bought a piece of fantasma. This isn't gold! Feel it! It's not heavy enough."

That gold (fantasma) bracelet became part of the wall décor. I put it in a frame with a boldly written note below that read:

DON'T ASK - THE ANSWER IS NO!!!

Consular officers and representatives are advised to clear out files every year, and destroy any file that's over five years old. I didn't always do this. Some case files were too interesting to destroy, and I'm glad I didn't. They came in handy sometimes.

Joseph Mahler was one of these. Get a picture of this. It was September in Puerto Vallarta. We were having the usual hot, muggy, steamy weather and Joseph walked into the Consular Agency. He was wearing a wool cap pulled low on his brow, and covering his ears. He was dressed in long ragged pants, the legs stuffed down into high-top shoes. He had a long-sleeved shirt on, which opened at the neck showing a grungy grey undershirt. He had a wool Macintosh jacket over this. His beard and moustache were as long and tangled as his shoulder-length hair. He stunk to high heaven.

He walked up to the counter and says, "I'm Joe. I'm ready to go home now."

"Where's home, Joe?" I asked him.

"Washington, D.C." he answered.

"What's your last name?"

"Mahler, Joseph Mahler. Joseph P. Mahler." He even spelled it for me.

The light bulb went on. I had recently been thumbing through old files, and ran across one I should have dumped, but I didn't. It was brief, and written in capital letters:

TO: ALL POSTS
FROM: CITIZENS EMERGENCY CENTER
DEPT. OF STATE
JOSEPH P. MAHLER, DPOB 11-24-43 WASHINGTON, D.C.
REPATRIATE DIRECT FROM ANYWHERE OUTSIDE
UNITED STATES OF AMERICA.

There was a street address in Washington, D.C. and a phone number.

You would be surprised what is donated to consular offices. I had crutches, walkers, and bits of soap, partially-used tubes of toothpaste, combs, clothes, shoes, and eyeglasses. I even had an empty portable oxygen tank, and they all came in handy. Especially the clothes.

I pulled out a clean change of clothes from my donated stash, and, gave him a bar of soap. My guard led him to the men's room in the basement to clean up. I told Rafael to leave the dirty clothes in the trash can in the basement.

I don't know who set up the fund or why, but the State Department kept an active Trust Fund for Joe, which provided him with money for food, and an airline ticket home whenever he wanted. He was a walker, and was well known throughout the consular offices in Nicaragua, El Salvador, Guatemala, Ecuador, and Mexico. He had been repatriated from all these countries.

The lady who cleaned the basement bathrooms didn't speak to me for a month. Joseph had left the men's room flooded, and she had to dispose of his stinking clothes.

About three years went by and Joe showed up at the office again. I recalled his stench before I recognized him. He simply said, "I'm Joe. I'm ready to go home now."

This time I gave him clean clothes, a bar of soap, and sent him to the river to bathe.

All Destitutes were not bums. Some truly had no place to go and nobody to ask for help. Others just didn't know how to look for help.

One poor soul was Lorraine. She came from St. Louis and traveled with a beautiful, red Irish setter. I guess her biggest problem was that she was lonely, cold, and disappointed in her life. One day she quit her job, packed a suitcase, hopped in her car with the Irish setter, and headed out for Mexico. She met a man on the way named Carlos, who offered to help her drive the Mexican highways.

They got as far as Puerto Vallarta when the car ran out of gas and Lorraine ran out of money. Carlos told her he had friends in town who could loan him enough money to fill the car with gas, and he would drive over to Yelapa, where he had family who would loan them some money. He had been gone two weeks and she was worried about him.

First of all, you couldn't get to Yelapa by road. It was only accessible by boat. It's not an island, but it's a costal village where no access roads had been built. It didn't have telephones or electricity. Communication with the outside world was by two-way radio. Lighting was by generators, candles, kerosene lamps, or battery operated devices.

Lorraine felt she and her dog had been abandoned, and they had. She would never see Carlos or her car again. She didn't have a job, didn't have relatives or friends she wanted to contact, but she wanted to go home. She had had to leave the cheap hotel where she was staying after Carlos left her. She recognized how gullible she had been, was ready to accept her mistakes, and go back to St. Louis, but she didn't have any money to get there.

She was agreeable to applying for a Repatriation Loan. She didn't know how she would repay, but she wanted to leave Puerto Vallarta. The big problem was the US government could repatriate Lorraine, but not her dog, and she wasn't going anywhere without her Irish setter.

This woman was Destitute, but Determined. I tried to keep a bowl of fruit on the front counter in the Consular Agency. I refused to have a coffee pot perking since that tended to attract the folks who had nothing to do, but sit around all day and chat. She and her dog were waiting for me every morning when I got to the office. She took one banana, peeled it, divided it in two, gave one piece to the dog, and ate the other. She put one apple in her pocket for later in the day. Her hair was always combed neatly, and the dog appeared to be freshly groomed. Perhaps they were bathing in the river also. Every morning we talked.

"Lorraine, give up," I pleaded. "I can find a home here for your dog, a good home. You can go back to St. Louis and start all over. This is not the end of the world. Give me your dog and I'll get you a ticket home." She refused.

She found a nook behind the gate between the cathedral and Padre Luis' office. She discovered she could sleep there safely. I gave her an old blanket, and she had the extra warmth of the brick walls of the church and her dog. We talked every morning, but she was adamant. She would not leave Puerto Vallarta without her dog. I went to see Padre Luis Ramirez and explained what I was up against. He said, "Leave her be. Things will take care of themselves." And Padre was right.

Lorraine got sick. The blanket, the dog and the sun warmed brick walls of the church were not enough to keep out the night cold. She wasn't eating well, and she shared what little she begged off the padre, market vendors, and me with her dog. FAM said I definitely could not bring folks like this into my home or allow them to sleep in the office, and I agreed with that FAM section.

One day another tourist phoned me. She said she had picked up Lorraine and her dog out on the highway near the airport. Lorraine had told this Good Samaritan how she happened to be in her predicament, and that she was hitchhiking back to the United States. She had driven Lorraine to a pharmacy, bought medicine for her cold, and then checked her into a cheap hotel where the manager allowed the dog to stay.

The lady told me, "I'm buying her a ticket home."

"But what about the dog?" I asked.

"I'm shipping the dog with her."

I never met Lorraine's rescuer, but we chatted for a good while on the phone. She said she wasn't concerned about ever being re-paid. She could afford to do this, and she hoped somebody would do the same for her if needed.

Do any of you remember Tom Brosnahan's book, *"Mexico on $20.00 a Day"?* I think the first one he came out with might have been *"Mexico on $5.00 a Day"*. That wasn't possible even in the 60's. Larry Rivera, one of my supervising consuls, used to claim that all these books should be banned from the market. Too many people believed they could actually travel in Mexico on $20.00 dollars a day, but few could.

One afternoon just at closing time, a family of four walked into the Consular Agency. There was a plump grey-haired grandmother wearing a wide-brimmed straw hat, which she had tied under her chin. Her dress was a Hawaiian muumuu, and she wore sandals. Her daughter, age thirty eight, was dressed exactly like her, but in a different colored muumuu. The two fat granddaughters, ages twelve and eight, wore the same garb as their mama and grandma. None of them had suitcases, but each carried two cardboard boxes tied with rope, which held everything they owned. They had been living in Hawaii, but found it too expensive. Grandma pulled a paperback book from the straw handbag she carried, and said,

"This ain't true here in Puerto Vallarta!"

The title of the book was *"Mexico on $20.00 a Day"*.

This family had no home to be repatriated to, but they did have a friend in San Antonio who was willing to give them bed and board for a while. All the necessary Repatriation Loan forms were filled out and signed, and they began their trip to Texas, still looking for a place they could live on $ 20.00 dollars a day.

Charles McClain really belongs in the Dirty Old Men chapter, but he was also a Destitute, and had no home. He had been homeless when he lived in the United States, so I guess he figured he could sleep on Mexican streets as well as he could on Philadelphia streets. The weather is certainly nicer, but Puerto Vallarta doesn't have Salvation Army or Goodwill soup kitchens.

However, it is amazing how long some of these people survive due to the goodness of the kind, generous Mexican. At one time Aurelio Vazquez operated a restaurant on Morelos Street. He offered to help out with food if we ever got in a bind. I sent several hungry people to him with my handwritten note asking that he feed them. We had agreed that they could dine, but not wine. The waiters at the Carlos O'Brian Restaurant have been known to slip a taco or two out the back door also. For many years Juanita de Muñoz operated a fruit and vegetable store across the street from the public market. She could be counted on for the occasional apple or orange. People in this country don't let folks starve to death.

McClain was a bum by nature, and a Destitute by profession. He didn't want to be repatriated anywhere. His life style was better than it had been in many years. He had obviously worked at something at one time in his life, since he had a Social Security monthly income of about $200 dollars.

He used the Consular Agency office as his mailing address. He was truly a pest around the first of each month. He would start coming to see me on the first Monday after the first day of the month. Charles tricked me into shaking hands with him one time. One time! He had palmed one of those icky lizards we call *cuizas* in his hand. He always brought a lizard to the office when he came, but I never shook hands with him again. Finally, one day he disappeared and no more checks came for him. I had to assume he moved on down the coast with his lizards.

Many Americans used to live in Mexico on their Social Security or Veteran's pensions. Before the US government encouraged pensioners to maintain a bank account in the U.S. so their checks could be directly deposited, people had serious financial problems at times.

FBU, Federal Benefits Unit, probably exists in our consulate generals and embassies throughout the world. We Americans tend to spread out. Back in The Old Days, these federal checks were sent from Wilkes-Barre, Pennsylvania to our embassies by diplomatic pouch. From there they were distributed to the consulate general offices, and then posted to the recipient by local snail mail. In our case it was The Burro Express. Mexican mail service is better than it used to be, but I have loaned many a dollar to a man waiting for his check to arrive.

The general rule was that it took the Social Security Administration offices in the United States three months to correct any information in their data base. That means if you didn't have a bank account in the US where your check could be directly deposited, you had better have enough money stashed back to get you through three months or more, when making a change in your address. One old man died on the banks of El Pitillal River while waiting for his Social Security check. When it did finally get here, it couldn't even be used to pay for his burial.

Traveling by bus throughout Mexico is a popular means of transportation. However, there are so many different classes of busses it is difficult to describe them all. We have ETN and Primera Plus, which rival Greyhound and Stagecoach. They are equipped with roomy comfortable reclining seats, and bathrooms. They even provide sandwiches and soda pops on some of the longer trips, and you might even get to watch a movie as you're riding along. We also have the blue line, red line, yellow line, and the chicken and pig line. The first-class busses are not supposed to pick up passengers after they have left the terminal, but they sometimes do, especially if they don't have an inspector riding along. You're liable to stop fifteen times along the roadside to pick up a passenger on any of the other lines. These tariffs are extra pocket money for the driver.

Armed bandits were notable all over Mexico in the 80's. Tour busses were the most popular target, and many people lost their cameras, jewelry, passports, tourist cards, credit cards, and cash in these hold-ups. I never thought long-distance scheduled busses would be a lucrative target, but they were.

I particularly remember this case because the boy was named Blue.

Twelve year old Blue Tennyson and his father came into the office one morning. They had been victims of an armed robbery as they traveled by bus from Guadalajara to Puerto Vallarta. You truly couldn't call them Destitutes because they called Blue's mother in the United States, and she wired them money to continue their trip.

Blue's father described the scene as scary.

Their bus left the terminal in Guadalajara on schedule. Outside of the city limits the driver pulled off the road to let a passenger on. He only rode a short distance before he asked to get off. The driver continued for a few more miles before stopping to pick up two more male passengers. Further down the road two more men were waiting to board the bus. They were carrying handguns, as were the last two who had boarded. There were two gunmen in the back of the bus and two in the front. They ordered all passengers to get off, walk into an empty field by the side of the road, and to lie face down on the ground.

The armed robbers took all jewelry, billfolds, purses, and carry-on luggage from the passengers. This was a well-planned robbery. The fifth accomplice drove up in a battered pick-up truck, the loot was loaded, and all five took off down the road, leaving the passengers still lying face down in the field.

Fortunately, the robbers didn't get into the luggage compartment of the bus, and the Tennysons had clean clothes.

Can't you just imagine what happened at Blue's school that fall when the teacher said, "It's Show-and-Tell Day. Let's hear about your summer vacation?"

CHAPTER SEVEN

Bureaucraps

We have all had to deal with them at one time or another. They are just as awful on the north side of the border as they are on the south side. I think I came very close to undergoing a body search in Houston one day. I decided to fly out for the weekend, and since I kept a wardrobe of clothes in Houston, I took very little with me in my carry-on bag.

The customs official who checked me in Houston was an overly portly woman who reeked of diesel fuel. She asked me, "What are you bringing with you out of Mexico?"

The only thing extra I had packed in my suitcase was a bag of those plastic-looking pinwheels you fry up in bacon fat, and they taste a bit like pork skins.

"Something that tastes like pork skins, but it is not pork."

"Pork skins!" she cried. "You can't bring pork skins into this country!"

I gritted my teeth and spit out the words, "I said it tastes like pork. It is not pork skins!"

She backed up a step, both arms akimbo on her hips, lowered her head toward her ample chest, and glared at me with her beady eyes. "Yeah, well. What did you pay for that *centenario* hanging around your neck?"

"That is not a *centenario*," I told her, "It is an Austrian *corona* and my husband gave it to me as a gift."

Still glaring at me, she ordered, "Step up here a little closer so I can get a better look."

I should have kissed her but, I whispered, "Look sister, we both work for the same government. Now please let me pass through this line." I showed her my identification card and she begrudgingly waved me on through with her search wand.

I have heard some horror stories of how our Mexican friends have been treated by our own customs and immigration officials and I can believe every word of it.

We start trembling the night before we come into this country, knowing that some customs official is going to run his dirty hands over our clean clothes in our suitcase. We are terrified he will find that stick of Genoa salami stuck inside a tennis shoe. Heaven help us if he decides to count the CDs or the packs of cigarettes.

Customs officials are child's play when compared to immigration officials. A visit to that office is a two-tranquilizer trip, at least. Hands sweating, dry mouth, pulse rate up about fifty beats above normal, you timidly hand in your papers proving you are legally in this country and request only a few more days of extension to tie up loose ends before departing. With a shy, hopefully ingratiating, smile you may even tender a brand new Mont Blanc pen, box of candy, bottle of perfume or a fine bottle of brandy, depending upon the presumed gender of the official. That is not a bribe. It is merely a token of your appreciation and life-long gratitude. Witches! All of them! Be they south or north of the border.

In the mid 80's I was invited to a meeting with a group of city officials, including the mayor, director of tourism and the top immigration official. This was BTS, Before Time Share. The young men who were presenting the proposal extolled the benefits this would bring to the city. It was likened to buying an apartment, but you only paid for two weeks rental per year, and somebody else would be responsible for the maintenance and upkeep. What fun it would be to go back home and tell friends you had bought a piece of paradise. They would be so envious that they would want a piece also. That way, the city collects more and more business dollars. And, repeat business at that.

Someone raised the questioned regarding employment. This matter had already been addressed behind doors other than the ones in this room. The Federal Employment Law states that a company can hire one foreigner for every ten Mexicans. The General Population Law, which is the mother law for Immigration Regulations, says that if the number of foreign employees does not affect the Mexican citizen for the same position, then the number of foreigners can be determined at discretion.

The number of foreign time-share employees fell into the "determined at discretion" mode. I looked around the room and saw the city fathers' heads nodding up and down in agreement.

"Why not?" I could just hear them thinking. "This could mean big bucks for the city coffers." I sat smiling smugly and thinking to myself, "Dream on, dummies! That will never happen! You won't ever find enough people stupid enough to do what you are proposing." Really smart back then, wasn't I? Time-Share Sales was born that day in Puerto Vallarta.

Somehow along the way, news got out in the United States and Canada that companies were hiring foreigners to work in sunny Puerto Vallarta, Mexico. If you could speak English and had the gift of gab of a used car salesperson and wore semi-nice clothes, you could qualify for the job.

There were notable exceptions and they stood above the crowd, but this notice brought in the biggest wave of foreign scum bags this country has ever seen; people who were drop-outs in their own countries. They were society mis-fits, ne'er do-wells, dope addicts and alcoholics. I met many of the early-comers when they were incarcerated and behind bars.

Construction began all along the coast. Modules popped up on every street corner. They were manned by young Mexican men and women. Some could even speak a smattering of English. They showed glossy pictures of automobiles and tour boats to you. They offered you Free Breakfast. "Hey, Mister, I got a deal for you!" was one of the first phrases they learned. The kicker was that if you opted for their deal on a Jeep rental, for example, you were required to sit through a condo time-share pitch before you received the car keys. If you went for the Free Breakfast, you had to sit through the pitch also. These kids were called OPCers. That means Outside Public Contact. .

All these employees had special titles. The person you encountered at your Free Breakfast was called a Liner. He or she was probably dressed a little finer than the OPCer. He certainly spoke fluent English.

Lots of free booze flowed at these Free Breakfasts. Your glass was never empty. They served you coffee laced with a heavy jolt of brandy, a Bloody Mary, a Mimosa or maybe a cold beer. Because it was Free, you keep on sipping. The Liner regaled you with the Owner's Benefits, and how you could lord it over your friends when you got back home that you had "bought a little place down there in Puerto Vallarta."

Everything he told you fell like music on your ears. It was exactly what you wanted to hear, but you didn't know if you could afford it. You expressed your doubt to Mr. Liner. Sold! He had you then! He sympathized with you, talked about the cost of living, but most importantly, talked about how imperative it is to live life to its fullest enjoyment.

He said to you, "I know exactly how you must feel and we would never want to be part of a financial burden on you. Why don't you give me your credit card and we will run a check on you, and see if your credit card company thinks you can do this?" You handed over your credit card, and he disappeared behind the door.

About thirty minutes passed by and you were sitting there wondering, "Is my credit truly that bad? Have I charged something I don't remember? What sort of limit do I have on this card? Perhaps I will need to use another card?" That is when Mr. Closer smoothly slipped in.

Mr. Closer probably looked as if he had just stepped from the Grooming Salon, hair perfectly cut, smoothed into a fashionable style, fingernails trimmed and buffed or polished to a high sheen. His shoes were definitely not tennis and his pants were definitely not Levis. He may or may not have been wearing a coat and tie, but one thing for sure was that he was wearing what looked like a gold Rolex watch. That was supposed to show how successful he was.

He congratulated you on being qualified to own your Corner of Paradise. You signed the contract, he handed your credit card back to you, and you and your mate, if you have one, walked euphorically out of there, and returned to your hotel to sleep and rest on your dream.

A hang-over cannot compare with Buyer's Remorse. Johnny's teeth braces have not been paid for. Sally still has two more years in college. The car needs new tires. You decided to cancel this agreement, and you went back to the scene of the crime, only to be told that your credit voucher was already being processed in the Cayman Islands and there was no cancellation clause in your contract.

That is where we met. You came to see me and pled your case. In most cases, I could not help you. I could not even help the elderly man who hobbled into the office one morning to report that one of those Closers had threatened to throw him off the roof terrace of a three-story building if he did not sign the contract.

As time went by and this enterprise grew, PROFECO, the Federal Protection of the Consumer Agency recognized a need to step in and offer protection to consumers of this product. Not only were foreigners being led into a twenty-year snare, but Mexicans were also becoming victims.

If you reported to PROFECO that you felt the time-share company had misrepresented the facts to you, or had used undue pressure or coercion to obtain your signature on a contract, they would usually go to bat for you.

It was a lengthy and bothersome process. Most of the time, you needed a translator, which PROFECO couldn't always provide. Your remaining vacation was ruined by anxiety over your chance of not recovering your money, not being able to communicate, and sitting around in another bureaucrap's office while the clerks munch on potato chips or file their fingernails.

To begin with, you could possibly fight this battle out with your credit card company, but they wised up. PROFECO could, and did, provide a service to the consumer. After much paper work, it cited the time-share company to make an appearance in PROFECO. At first, the companies tended to ignore this citation. PROFECO cited again. If a representative from a time-share company did not make an appearance, a hefty fine was imposed on the company. That began to get their attention.

Sometimes, the consumer sought local legal advice and brought suit against the company, which got even more attention. The slime balls who worked for these companies could care less for this inconvenience. The OPCer, the Liner and the Closer had already received their commission and probably spent most of it. The company could recuperate some of this money, if the person continued to work, by reducing his next pay check.

There are exceptions to every rule. Fernando and Kistner were the exceptions in time-share. I tried to keep from asking them special favors. They never failed me when I did ask. If they employed one or more of these slime balls, and could see there was something salvageable underneath all the scum, they tried to save them. They sent the nerds to detoxification centers, involved them in self-help programs, and in general, tried to promote a better self-image within these pieces of human good-for-nothings. Sometimes they succeeded, sometimes all failed, but they made the effort. I will always be grateful to them for their attempt to make the world rosier.

Even though immigration authorities had made it possible for the foreigners to be legally employed, many of them started working without fulfilling the necessary requirements. Before they could begin the process they needed a U. S. passport, but legality was a word many had never paid too much attention to in the first place, so they began working anyway.

Immigration inspectors were aware of this, so they also availed themselves of the Free Breakfast. They would leave their uniform at home the day they went for breakfast. They blended in with the rest of the suckers, and all the inspectors had to do was present their credentials; ask Mr. Liner for his FM-3, the document, which allowed him to work legally. If he couldn't show his FM-3, he could pay a substantial fine, and plead that it was *"en tramite"*, being processed.

Another day came when I needed to smile prettily, act pigeon-toed, and put on my best dress to visit the immigration office. Maybe that was the day I started taking high blood pressure medicine, I don't recall. I sat in my chair, with hands sweating, mentally reviewing what to say to get my message across to make them understand I needed Immigration's help in deporting a fugitive from justice in the USA. I had never done such a thing. My job requirements stated I was supposed to aid the American citizen in whatever way was possible. I had never dealt with hard-core criminals, but I was here on an assignment by the Federal Bureau of Investigation.

The Chief of Immigration called me into his office and closed the door behind us. He laid his head against the wall, then battering the wall with his fists, cried, "Aiii yaiiii yaiiii, Juanita, what am I going to do with all these people of yours who are working down here illegally?" I put my hand on his shoulder and sympathized with him, "I don't know, Chief. We have the same problem with your folks up north."

CHAPTER EIGHT

Dos Morticians

I met Ignacio and Angelina's oldest daughter at her fifteenth birthday party. Last week, at twenty-six, she got married. The reception was held for five hundred guests in the most elegant hotel in the city. There can be a good living in all walks of life, even in the body business.

The first time I met Ignacio was in Judge Salazar's chambers. An American man had been piloting his small plane over the jungle area near Mismaloya, the next little village down the coast from Puerto Vallarta. Accompanying him was his daughter. A sudden wind draft caused the plane to crash through the trees before it hit the ground. Daughter was, miraculously, thrown from the plane and landed in a palm tree. The father did not fare so well. Ignacio boxed the broken body in a coffin and shipped it back to the United States via Aeroméxico airlines. The charge for transportation and his service was $1,500 dollars. The daughter wrote him a check, but stopped payment on it when she returned home.

Ignacio filed a court action against her and it was eventually kicked back to the Mexican courts. That day I promised him he would never have this problem again as long as he and I were working together. Many years passed before he accepted credit cards, but he never took another personal check.

The next time we met was on the death case of Dana. She and her fiancé, Fred, had come to the beach to do some deep sea exploration before continuing on to Florida to meet her parents. She took some lessons from an instructor in their hotel swimming pool before going out in a boat. They had made several successful dives and were quitting for the day. Then they decided to go down for one last look.

Dana came up too quickly and got the bends. The USS Mobile was in the bay at the time, so the boat driver sped toward the big vessel with the hopes a decompression chamber might be on board. There wasn't one.

Fred was crying as he gave me the details and I was crying as I filled out my Report of an American Citizen's Death Abroad form. Twenty seemed too young to die. They were handsome, fun-loving kids on their way to beginning a married life together. I don't know who was doing the most comforting that day; him or me.

Later I went by Ignacio's back room of his house, where he had set up his funeral parlor, to make sure he had registered the death with Civil Registry office, so we would be free to ship the body back to the United States with a Mexican death certificate.

I knocked on the door, but nobody answered. I called out for him and still nobody answered. I pushed the door open and froze. There lay Dana in a slanted concrete trough with an open drain down close to her feet. She had been hosed down; her long, blonde hair was slicked back and brushed out around her head. She was dressed the same as the day she came out of her mother's womb.

Ignacio must have heard me gasp or moan, because he came stumbling into the room as if he had been awakened from a much needed sleep.

I'm not sure how Ignacio survived and ended up such a money-making mortician, but I have a pretty good idea. He never had much competition. An early competitor was Mr. Villegas.

One night there was a multiple auto accident out on the highway towards the Diaz Ordaz airport north of town. I had been called to the hospital late in the evening. There were injured folks all over the place. Some bodies had already been taken to the two funeral parlors. I was slipping in blood as I rushed from broken bones to head injuries, to eyeballs lying on cheekbones, arms being slit open to insert catheters, to the final groans of agony from departing souls.

Ignacio and Villegas were standing out in the hallway in contemplation of who would get the next body. It was late, I was tired and I was very saddened by what I had witnessed this evening. Mrs. Villegas cleared the slate for me in her own way.

Mr. Villegas's funeral parlor differed from Ignacio's in that it was in the front room of his house. Ignacio's funeral parlor in the back room of his house had only a curtain separating his old grey metal desk from the cement trough. Mr. Villegas had two rooms. He kept his supply of coffins in the room that opened onto the main street. Inside that room was a stairway leading up to his living quarters. Behind the room full of coffins was another little room where he had a cement ice chest built big enough to hold a body. There is where he did cadaver preparations. In order to enter his living quarters, he had to go thorough the coffin room.

On the night of our multiple disasters, Mrs. Villegas turned all the lights off and climbed into one of the coffins to wait for her tippling husband to come home. At the moment he entered the pitch dark house, she raised herself up out of the coffin and loudly whispered, "This is the last time you'll come creeping in here late at night, old man." That gave him such a shock he took to his bed and never drank another drop.

One of the stories Ignacio and I love to tell at parties is about the time we took ashes for disposal at sea.

I was contacted by a funeral director in the United States, inquiring how to go about carrying out his client's last wishes. He had visited Puerto Vallarta many times. He died in Kentucky, but wanted his ashes buried at sea on our coastline. We figured out the best way would be for the stateside funeral director to ship the ashes directly to Ignacio. Ignacio would call me when they arrived and we would go down the coast a way, rent a motorized flat-bottomed boat and do our duty. This was the first time either of us had done anything like this in our line of work, but it seemed the reasonable and logical thing to do.

Ashes arrived in September. Ignacio called and we made arrangements for him to pick me up early one morning and off we would go with the ashes in his rust-eaten, worn-out old station wagon.

So far, so good. We got to the village of Mismaloya, but all the *pangas* had already been rented, so we traveled on down the road to the next fishing village, Boca de Tomatlan. There we hired a fisherman to take us out in his little boat. The waves carried us from shore to the sandbar. Bigger waves floated us on out to deeper water where we would crank the *panga* up and be off to work.

Our boatman yanked that crank cord until the veins in his neck were bulging and sweat was pouring from his face. All the motor did was sputter as we floated further and further out to sea. The more the boat rocked, the sicker I got. I looked over at Ignacio and he was as white-faced as I. I muttered to him, "If I'm not mistaken I have a Dramamine in my *bolsa.*" I had only one pill for the two of us. I bit it in two and gave half to him. We swallowed without the benefit of a washer-down.

About the time we had decided we were going to end up like the ashes crated in a cardboard box setting on the wooden plank between us, a fisherman from Las Animas, the next village down the coast, came by, saw our distress and threw a rope out to us.

As we were being towed back into shore, Ignacio said, "Not to worry. *No problema.* As soon as we get there, we'll rent another boat, go out and try it again."

My answer was a resounding, "Oh, no we won't! Dump those ashes right now!" He did and we later received a proper warning from the naval authorities. We were dumping pollutants within the twelve-mile zone and tropical Agatha was forming off our coastline.

From that time on, we asked for a naval escort when we went to sea to dump ashes.

Another one of our trips to the cemetery was the day Dorothy Vance died. Dorothy was a dear little old lady who lived in a house on the most popular beach in town, Los Muertos. She called her house Casa de Buen Hombre. She had a rose garden in front of her house, which she kept immaculately clipped. On the days she didn't feel up to clipping her rose garden, her maid did it for her.

Dorothy was a movie star. She had been one of the school teachers on the bus Richard Burton drove through town when *The Night of the Iguana* was filmed in Puerto Vallarta. Dorothy knew one joke, which she told at every cocktail party she attended.

She would say, "Dew yew know why Mister and Mizzes Sandy Claws newver had any children?"

For the twentieth time, you would politely say, "No, Dorothy, I don't. Why was that?"

She would cackle, "Because Mister Sandy Claws newver came but wunz a year and then he went off up the chimney."

I don't know if this other story is true or not, but I always heard it was. There was a time when there were no banks in Puerto Vallarta. Señor Peña owned a dry goods store on Juarez Street, and he would cash checks for foreigners. If you had valuables you wanted stored in a safety deposit box, you had to do business with a bank in Guadalajara. At one time, Dorothy needed a safety deposit box.

One day her husband died in his chair by the window where he liked to sit, and watch the people walk along the beach. She put a bed sheet around him, and tied him to the chair so he wouldn't tumble out. She hopped on a bus to Guadalajara, got what she needed from the safety deposit box, rode a bus back to Puerto Vallarta, and only then, did she report her husband's death to the proper authorities.

I heard that before Dorothy died, she had given away most of her jewelry and spent the majority of her wealth. She used it while she had it. Her daughter, Betty, had little left for a coffin.

Bob and Elena Gollum, Betty and I were following the old, battered, black pick-up truck that was carrying Dorothy's body. I don't know how it is now, but that road was unpaved, full of pot-holes and very bumpy then. Betty had chosen a faded grey velvet covered casket for her mother. It was draped all around with a three-inch fringe. The fringe was doing a jitter-bug dance as we rocked along the bumpy road. By the time we reached the cemetery, most of it had come loose, and was only held to the casket in two or three spots. However shabby the casket may have been, Betty had brought along a basket of beautiful pink roses from Dorothy's garden to lay on her grave. She gave each of us a rose.

We were in a somber mood on our way back into town until the talk of another death came up when Elena asked me, "What's the news on that girl who was shot in Paso Ancho last night?"

I told her, "It wasn't Paso Ancho. She was shot in El Pitillal."

Betty cried out, "Shot in the what?" That crack resolved all somberness. We laughed so hard that Bob couldn't even drive the car. He pulled up to a roadside stand and bought cold beers for all of us. Dorothy would have loved it!

It was a beautiful Easter Sunday morning that turned into a nightmare for many folks. I received a telephone call from one of the hospitals that a man and his wife had been shot out on the golf course. The husband was in the hospital, but his wife was dead. Howard and I took off for the hospital.

I interviewed the man who was not critically wounded, although he did have a bullet lodged in his lung, and another went through his arm. He told me he was a dentist from Des Moines, and he and Doreen, his wife, were on their honeymoon in Puerto Vallarta. He said a young, clean-faced Mexican boy had appeared from the trees on the 7th hole, and approached them, carrying his own golf club bag. Dr. Peters thought the kid was asking him for the time of day when he pointed to the watch on his arm. He told him it was 10:30, but the boy shook his head and said, "Money."

"I had left my wallet and credit cards with our passports and tourist cards in the locker room. I had $1.87 in my pocket. I gave that to him, and turned my pockets inside out to show him I had nothing left. I bent over to pick up my bag, and put it back in the cart when I heard two loud gun shots ring out. I spun around to see Doreen lying on the ground, covered with blood, and the boy holding a rifle. He quickly fired two more times at me, and then ran back into the trees. I crawled to Doreen. I thought she must be dead. There was no movement, she wasn't breathing, and I couldn't hear her heart beating. I managed to drive the golf cart to the club house to get help, leaving Doreen lying on the greens," he told me.

"Do you remember how you got here to the hospital?" I asked.

"Somebody from the club house brought me in his truck."

"Do you think you could identify the man if the police can find him?"

"I believe I could. He's not a man, just a young boy. A teen-ager, I would say. He didn't look as if he had ever shaved. His face was clean as a baby's."

I tucked one of my business cards into his hands, and asked him to tell me the most important thing I could do for him at that moment. He told me to go find his wife's body. So the Big Chase began.

I called Ignacio to meet us at the golf course since I thought that was where the body would be. The employees at the club house were hesitant to give us any information. As far as they were concerned, we represented the law, and nobody wanted to get involved. Finally, one man nodded to the north and quietly said, "San Juan."

None of us bothered to ask, "Which San Juan?" There is San Juan and there is San Juan de Abajo. Then there are San Juan de Valle and San Juan de Los Ángeles. These little San Juan villages are fairly close together, but they are all located down different roads leading off from the main highway.

We found a man, leaning back in a chair, propped under a shade tree in the first San Juan. He wore khaki pants and matching shirt. The only identification he wore was the pistol strapped to his thigh. He had heard about this shooting over his radio, but he thought the body must have been taken to San Juan de Los Angeles. At least, that's where the district attorney's office was, and that would probably be the proper place to take a body on an Easter Sunday afternoon.

On one of those dirt roads, a state police car overtook us and the driver motioned for us to pull off to the side. He was a man I had known for many years, and at one time had been a security guard at the international airport. I don't know how many years it had been since anyone had seen this man's eyes. His dark wrap-around sunglasses and a big unlit cigar in his mouth were his official badge. The rumor was the man was the "Mafioso boss" in this part of the state. His mission that day was to direct us to the correct San Juan while he vowed, "I'll find this killer for you, *Señora.*"

Doreen was wrapped in a sheet, and lying on the end of the front porch to the shack used as the office of the district attorney. It was already a hot day in the tropics, and the flies were swarming the bloody sheet. I walked into the shack, and found the district attorney and his assistant eating a watermelon, and intensely watching a soccer match on a huge, color television.

I walked back onto the porch, and instructed Ignacio and his workers to load Doreen into his station wagon and head back to Puerto Vallarta.

That broke up the soccer game and brought the district attorney and his side-kick to the porch in a hurry. What I had not counted on was that we were taking a cadaver from the state of *Nayarit* across the state line into *Jalisco.* That was worse than robbing a grave. The shooting had happened in their state, and the officials meant they were going to get to do the paper work. They wanted to get the credit for working a crime that happened on their turf. After much haggling, sweet-talking, "waving of the flag", and reassuring them I would return the next day to give them the details for their reports, they agreed to allow us to take Doreen. There was a ladies' leather handbag lying beside Doreen's body.

I asked, "Is that hers?"

The district attorney nodded affirmatively.

"Then I'll take it with me," I told him.

He shrugged his shoulders nonchalantly, and walked back inside his hut.

When I returned home, and emptied Doreen's handbag to make an inventory, I learned why the district attorney didn't put up a fight over me taking it. All it contained was a pair of bloody sunglasses with one lens broken and an envelope of fabric swatches. I was able to recover her wedding rings from the district attorney when I returned to San Juan de Los Angeles the next day.

This particular case dragged on for many months. *Nayarit* police did arrest a young man whom they thought might be guilty. His photograph was sent to Dr. Peters who identified him as his wife's assassin. The boy was held in prison almost a year before Dr. Peters was summoned to Compostela, *Nayarit* for a face-to-face with him. I went with the doctor, and we invited Aurelio Vazquez to come along with us. Yeyo spoke very good English and Spanish. Although he was not what is called a *perito traductor,* he acted as our translator that day. It was scary.

I felt the judge was unfair and biased against us from the moment we walked into his office, which was the court room. He didn't want Yeyo to translate, albeit he couldn't speak English, and Dr. Peters spoke no Spanish. He didn't even want me in the same room. The defendant was surrounded with friends and family. I felt we were on very unfriendly territory.

Finally, the judge begrudgingly allowed us to participate in the hearing. He even took a formal statement from me. He stopped me abruptly in my recounting when I was saying, "…she was shot two times…"

"How do you know she was shot?" he demanded to know.

"Dr. Peters said he heard two gun shots. The deceased had a hole through one eye and another in her throat. The pathologist's report stated her death was caused by a .22 caliber projectile, and a bullet of that same size was found lodged in her husband's lung. Therefore, it is assumed she was shot with a weapon we call a rifle, Señor Juez."

The entire time we were sitting in the judge's chamber, the accused sat with his legs crossed, bent over with one elbow propped on his knee, gently stroking two whiskers protruding from his chin, which were about an inch long.

The kid was acquitted, and released that same afternoon while we were traveling back to Puerto Vallarta. He was later re-arrested, and sentenced to twelve years in prison.

All for $1.87 on a clear Easter morning.

Hundreds and hundreds of times, we sent out search and recovery teams for bodies lost and found at sea or in the mountains, picked up those who had jumped or fallen from tall hotel windows or terraces, over dosed or hanged themselves in their hotel rooms, got in line of the stray or purposeful bullet, automobile accident victims, doctor's over-zealous injections, or plain old natural deaths.

Ignacio was much more than our friendly local mortician. One night I was driving home alone from a reception given for a visiting US Navy vessel. A car drove up along side me and the driver called out, "*Señora*, you have a flat tire."

I recognized him as Dr. Pedro, a young doctor from one of our hospitals. We pulled off to the side of the highway; got out of our cars and inspected my tire. I asked him, "What am I to do, Doc? I don't know how to change a tire, you probably don't either, and it's too late at night to find a *llantera* open."

He advised me, "Leave it here for the night. Ignacio will take care of it tomorrow and bring your car to you. I'll take you home now."

Another time I went shopping with Marg Tolton, Lynn Nokes, and Missy Case. We had a hilarious day, whooping it up in one of the shops in the Bath-and-Body Zone of downtown Guadalajara. All of us bought good-smelling, greasy bath oils and satin bed sheets. It was Sunday afternoon when Howard fell out of bed.

I stood in a hallway outside the operating room while Howard was having his broken ankle repaired. Again, Dr. Pedro appeared. He asked why I was there. I told him, and expressed my concern over getting Howard back home and up three flights of stairs to our bedroom.

"Not to worry, *Señora*. *No problema*. Ignacio will take care of it."

As luck would have it, Ignacio came along to pick up yet another cadaver ... and at that precise moment Howard was being rolled out of the operating room. The first thing Howard saw was the funeral director and me leaning against the wall. He raised himself up off the gurney and said, "Not yet, Ignacio. Go look for somebody else. I'm not yours yet!"

CHAPTER NINE

Dios' Medicine Men

Some people claim that Dioscorides (40 A.D) was the Father of Anesthetics. He certainly wrote enough books about what he learned while he was running around with Nero and his troops, but it appears that Mexico had the same herbs and medicinal plants as Old Dio did.

Juniper berry? Isn't that what is used in making Gilbey's Gin? Cumin? We call it *cominos* down here and we use it in making our Chile con Carne. Castor oil? This country is loaded with castor bean plants and locals consider them to be an unsightly weed. We know it is poisonous, but we used it as a decorative plant in our garden in Texas. Dioscorides used all of these.

Our friend, Ralph Todesca, fell off a horse and broke his back while riding up in the mountains behind Puerto Vallarta. He lay moaning and groaning on the ground as he waited for a truck to come pick him up and take him to a doctor.

A native woman came out of her palm-thatched shack with a bottle of tequila. Ralph thought she was going to give him a drink of it, but that was not the case. She poured a shot of it in his navel! He swore his pain eased immediately.

It makes good sense. After all, tequila is made from a plant, as are many of our current medicines of choice.

I was an eye witness to some of this primitive medicine. Although Jane Ober suffered from Parkinson's disease, she never missed a brunch, lunch or cocktail party as long as Phil was alive. She also wrote a weekly column for Mexico's leading daily English newspaper, Mexico City News. Before retiring to Puerto Vallarta she had been on the staff of Los Angeles Times. She wrote about food, but I never saw any evidence she knew any more about cooking other than to stick a slice of Bimbo white bread in a pop-up toaster. Phil and the maids did all the cooking, but when Jane could control her fingers, she could type about Puerto Vallarta gossip.

About once a year *The News* invited all its correspondents to Mexico City for a three-day conference and a special awards dinner. Jane told me she complained to her table partner at the dinner about a problem she was having with a Plantar's wart on the bottom of her foot. She had it surgically removed by a doctor in Los Angeles, but it had become infected in Puerto Vallarta. She had been to several local doctors, but they hadn't been able to clear up the infection.

The lady at the table with Jane said, "Sounds to me as if you need a cleansing."

Jane asked, "What do you mean? A cleansing? I soak my foot every day in warm soapy water!"

"No, not that kind of cleansing. Have you never heard of a *brujo*? A witch doctor?"

"We have several witch doctors in Puerto Vallarta, but I don't think they call themselves that."

"Ask your maid about a *curandero,* one who cures. I'll bet she knows of one."

Sure enough, Jane came home from her conference and asked her Popea if she knew of a *brujo* in our area. Indeed, Popea knew one and agreed that Jane could probably benefit from a cleansing. I was the designated driver.

One morning the three of us piled in my car and we headed out north past the airport. I had no idea where we were going, but Popea assured us she knew how to get there. We crossed the Ameca River separating *Jalisco* and *Nayarit* states.

"Aw, Popea, are we going all the way to Tepic, *Nayarit*?" I asked her.

"We'll soon be there," she promised. We saw a sign pointing to Jarretaderas, and she directed me to make a left turn. Jarretaderas was more of a settlement than a village. We drove along a dusty dirt road, passing a few houses along the way. We came around a curve and saw about a dozen cars and pick-up trucks parked near a huge rubber tree. There must have been thirty people; men, women and children of all ages standing or sitting around the tree, or leaning against their vehicles. There were five or six folding chairs which were occupied, but an old man offered his chair to Jane when he saw her wobbling on her walking stick.

About twenty feet away from the tree was a fairly new brick building. It was built in a square shape and measured probably no larger than twelve by twelve feet. There was one door and the two windows were small and near the ceiling.

A man moseyed through the crowd of people selling small brown squares of cardboard. Each cardboard square had a number hand printed on it.

Popea told us, "He's selling *fichas*. That's a ticket to get inside."

We each pulled out the equivalent of fifty cents and bought our entry *ficha* and stood back to wait our turn.

It was not a long wait until the door opened and people started pouring out of the square building. All except one woman who looked to be in her fifties. A younger man and woman were on either side of her holding onto her arms.

The older woman was saying, "No, no, no, I can't get out the door. She has it blocked! I can't get out!"

"*Mamá*, the door is open. There's nothing blocking it. Look at me! There's nothing there." The daughter waved her arm through the open door to show her mother that it was clear. The woman put one foot out as if to walk out the door and abruptly stopped.

"No!" she cried. "See! My foot won't go through the door. I'm telling you, she has it blocked!"

This woman had the waiting crowd outside in suspense.

"Somebody's put a hex on her!" whispered a voice nearby.

"Her husband's cheating on her," another said. "It's the other woman who has blocked the door. She can't leave!"

It seemed as if the woman imagined there was a half-door blocking her passage, but the upper half of the door was open. She stuck her arm through the door, but her feet would not budge.

"Come on, mamá," the young man told her, "we're going out the door."

She came out the door, but she didn't walk out. If I had not seen this with my own eyes, I would never believe what I'm about to tell you. The young man and woman still had hold of her arms. Both of her feet lifted behind her at the same time. It appeared that she was being dragged over an unseen obstacle about three feet high. When she passed through the doorway, her feet lowered to the ground and she walked normally over to a pick-up truck. I saw it. Jane saw it. Popea saw it, as well as about thirty other people.

It was our turn to go into the brick building. It was hot and dark inside. It smelled of sweaty bodies and cheap cologne. There was a square table covered with a brightly embroidered tablecloth in the center of the room. There was a framed picture of Jesus Christ on the table and a candle was burning alongside it. The table also held a pitcher of water, a drinking glass, several small bottles of oils, a package of matches and that awful sweet smelling cologne, which is sold in every grocery store and drug store in Mexico, *La Flor de Naranja*. It's supposed to smell like orange blossoms. Phew! It stinks! Added to a crowded room of nervous sweating bodies, it stunk even worse. The walls were bare except for a framed shape of a heart, which looked to be made of red chenille balls. There was only one chair provided for the person being cleansed. The rest of us stood around the room.

Fortunately, Jane was not the first to be treated or we would have run for our lives when Marcelo, the *curandero,* started to work on her.

The first patient was a tiny crying baby. The parents told Marcelo the child had been crying non-stop for forty-eight hours. You'd think after that length of time, it would be too tired to cry, but he filled the room with his loud wailing. Marcelo motioned for the mother to sit in the chair, holding her baby.

He poured himself a glass of water and drank it. He placed his hands on the mother's head and began, what I suppose was his prayer. I assumed he was praying, but I didn't see anybody cross themselves and nobody had their eyes closed. They were all as bug-eyed as I. He took his hands off the mother's head, but continued praying while he motioned for her to take the clothes off the baby's chest. When the baby was undressed, Marcelo reached for one of the bottles on the table. He poured a small portion of oil into his palm, dipped his forefinger into the oil and made the sign of the cross on the baby's forehead and on its chest. Then he motioned for the mother to turn her baby over. Again, dipping his finger into the oil, he made the sign of the cross on the back of its neck, on both little shoulders and a big one in the middle of its back. There was silence in the room. The baby stopped crying. We were in awe, but Marcelo had not finished his act yet.

He reached for another bottle and poured its contents in a circle around the mother and her child seated in the chair. Then he dropped a lighted match onto the circle! A low burning circle of blue fire surrounded the chair. It burned out in less than thirty seconds and the baby remained quiet.

Jane and I discovered we were hanging on to each other for dear life. Her eyes were as big as saucers and our mouths were hanging wide open. She was next.

I said, "Don't worry, Jane. I'll be right behind you."

Popea and I helped her into the chair as Popea explained to Marcelo what problems Jane was having. He nodded, took another drink of water, made a circle with his hands and put them around Jane's head. He prayed for a few minutes, and while still praying, reached for the bottle of oil he had used on the baby. "Oh, no!" I'm thinking. "Surely he wouldn't expect Jane to strip to the waist!"

He poured the oil into his palm, dipped his forefinger into it and made the sign of the cross on her forehead and the back of her neck. He motioned for her to pull up her pants legs to above her knees and to place her hands, palms down, over her thighs. He dipped into the oil again and made the sign of the cross on her knees and the back of her hands. He motioned for Popea to re-arrange her pants. He reached under the table and pulled out branches cut from a chinaberry tree. He sprinkled that awful smelling cheap cologne on the branches and began sweeping Jane from top of the head down to her toes. After each stroke, he would shake the branches as if to rid them of fleas and sweep her again. He plucked one of the red chenille balls from the heart shape and gave it to her. He told her, "Adios," and we walked back out into the sunshine to the car. Jane had forgotten her walking stick.

We went back to see Marcelo two or three more times and the routine was always the same. He prayed and swept her down with chinaberry tree branches sprinkled with *La Flor de Naranja,* but she never got the ring of blue fire treatment.

We agreed we would never talk to our friends about exactly what took place in Marcelo's little brick building.

I later found out this man was well known in our city. Supposedly, some of the priests in our area would consult with him on occasion. I also heard that a man who later became city mayor was a frequent visitor to Marcelo.

Puerto Vallarta can proudly point to several modern, well equipped, expertly staffed hospitals. That was not always the case.

Driving south from the airport, cross over the bridge, leave the paved highway and just before you hit the cobblestones entering town, look over to your right. You'll probably still see rags of different sizes and colors hanging over a drying-line. That used to be the main birthing clinic in the city. It was run by two women.

A breathe of fresh air came to town when Doctora Iris, the Colombian, set up practice. Oh, what a sight to see! She was petite, gloriously sun-tanned, and pretty and spoke English. Her medical uniform was a crisp, clean, tight fitting white T-shirt worn with a pair of white Hot Pants. Hot Pants had to cover the navel, but they were supposed to show the crease that divided the buttock from the thigh. I never saw so many healthy, strong young men get as sick as they did when they learned about Dra. Iris Battleson. She made house calls on a Honda motorcycle.

Dra. Iris hooked up with two men doctors. One has already had enough written about him to fill a book and I've heard that the other one died with AIDS.

These three doctors opened what they called a *Sanatorio Medico*. If you didn't know better, you might think the word *sanatorio* indicated sanitary conditions. Think again!

An elderly gentleman fell on his head from the second floor of the public market as he was coming down the stairs. His wife called to tell me what had happened and that he was in the Sanatorio Medico

That day was my first visit to that hospital. There was nobody at the reception desk, no nurses in the hall, and no visitors in the lobby, nobody anywhere. There were no plaques on the doors to identify what might be behind them, so I went exploring.

I climbed the stairway to the second floor and I still didn't see anybody. I walked through a pair of swinging doors and found myself on a sunny outside terrace overlooking a rubbish heap below. There was a square wooden table on the terrace. Needles and syringes were laid out neatly on the table to dry. A little girl sat at the table playing. She was picking up those needles, one by one, and jabbing them into the table. Her mother-nurse appeared from another door and I told her I was looking for the American. She directed me to Mr. Hutchinson's room.

He was alone when I entered and either asleep or in a coma. He was hooked up to an intravenous solution, but the needle had come out of the vein and the solution was dripping into his arm, which was about twice the size it should have been. I went looking for the nurse. She was nowhere to be found. I guess she had taken her little girl home.

I knew there had to be somebody else in the hospital. I walked the halls knocking on doors and calling out. *"Hola! Hola! Buenas tardes! Anybody here?"* I opened a door and there sat the two male doctors playing backgammon. Mr. Hutchinson died later that evening.

Months passed before I had to make another visit to the non-sanitary hospital. Jerome Spencer was living down the coast in Yelapa and had been laid low with a bad case of salmonella. His friend, Johana Villafranca, was working in the Tourist Bureau and she heard about how ill he was, so she sent a *panga* for him. She got him into the hospital, and then called me.

Jerome was indeed ill and his state of illness made me ill. He was frail and his skin was sallow. There was a tray table by the side of his bed, which held a plate of the leftovers from his lunch. Setting next to the plate was a full bed pan. The flies couldn't make up their minds which to go after first.

Social Security Hospital existed, after a fashion. That facility was for Mexicans and only in rare emergencies would a foreigner be admitted there. That too, has changed. These days a foreigner can pay an annual fee to join the Mexican Social Security system and receive treatment.

We also had the Red Cross Hospital, but it was poorly staffed and mainly took care of cuts and bruises, but it had an ambulance. We would often see it at some outlying beach on a family outing.

It was somewhere in the mid seventies when Dr. Jose Romo came to town and made waves in this tranquil, scummy, fly-buzzed, medical frog pond.

He opened his office in downtown Puerto Vallarta on Morelos Street. People were dumbfounded with what they saw when they entered the front door. It was clean! The upholstery on the chairs was not torn, the walls were painted a clean white, the floor was immaculately swept and mopped, and nicely framed pictures hung at the proper position on the walls. They may have been framed cut-outs from magazines. I don't know, but they looked nice. The doctor was clean shaven, perfectly groomed from the top of his head down to his shiny shoes. He always wore a spotlessly clean white jacket. And he spoke Spanish, German and English.

Probably the worst thing Dr. Romo did to annoy the older Dr. Frogs was to install a mobile phone in his Volkswagen Bug. They didn't think of it first. One particular Dr. Frog complained to me that Romo was charging too much for his fees. My response was, "My Goodness, Doctor, I didn't realize there was a syndicate that controlled doctors' fees here."

Dr. Romo held his own in the original medical community and later opened Servicios Medicos de la Bahia, still operating across the highway from the Sheraton Hotel.

Regional Hospital was then built. It was a tri-government operation, funded by the city, state, and federal governments. Newspapers reported that it opened too soon because there wasn't enough money to operate it. Equipment and supplies were short. It had no ambulance and only five bed pans.

Another new young doctor moved to town. I don't remember exactly how we met him, but Dr. Eleazar Carrazco was on the staff at Regional Hospital. We had long talks about the needs of the new hospital.

Jane Ober was growing frailer by the day. Dr. Eleazar needed a place to live and Jane's friends thought she no longer should live alone. It worked perfectly and started a trend among the older foreign widows. This arrangement helped several young doctors make it through the 'lean years'. One of them is now a leading cardiologist in Puerto Vallarta. We had fun in those days, didn't we, Dr. George?

Remember Ralph? The guy with the shot of tequila in his navel? He hosted a party and we raised enough money to buy a used Chevrolet van. We had it converted into an ambulance, which we donated to Regional Hospital. The driver wrecked it on the first trip to a hospital in Guadalajara. We didn't gather enough money to have it fixed for over a year.

In the meantime, our US Navy ships were visiting more often, many times bringing Operation Handclasp with them. One shipment contained stretchers, walkers, crutches, gallons of cleaning supplies, grosses of disposable baby diapers and fifty bed pans. These were distributed between Red Cross and Regional Hospitals. The day after this delivery was made there was not a baby diaper in either hospital.

Then the Villanueva boys and their wives graduated from medical school and moved to Puerto Vallarta. They bought an old house on Basilio Badillo Street and hung a shingle, which read: *Centro Medico Quirugico*. These four doctors worked long, hard hours and invited other young doctors to join them. The old house grew into the four-story building it is today. The new CMQ Hospital north of downtown is another state-of-the-art facility.

I don't know which one of them had the idea to open a drug store, but it was a smart move. On a recent drive, I noticed only one CMQ drug store sign south of town, but there must be a hundred in town and half that many more on up the coastline to the north.

Medasist Hospital followed close behind CMQ and I think there must have been strong competition between the two hospitals. There shouldn't have been because Puerto Vallarta was growing fast. The Marina area was developing; hotels and condos were popping up all over the place. We had, at least, six commercial flights coming in from the United States every day and charters were arriving from Canada. We had four cruise ships coming every week. We were bulging at the seams and needed both of these modern hospitals with their young doctors.

The truly rewarding thing to see develop in this budding medical community was the fact that the young men and women were chasing the old pill-pushing frogs and they had to shape up or get out. Most of them got out.

After we passed the millennium, first-class diagnostic clinics with high-tech equipment came into being. Santa Teresa, San Javier, Amerimed and Cornerstone Hospitals opened their doors.

There still are medical evacuations out of Puerto Vallarta, but fewer than in the old days. You see, this new generation is much smarter than the old one in many ways. They know their medicine, but they also know their limitations.

My hat is off to every one of these women and men. I've seen some of them grow up from the time their mamas were still walking them to school, holding them by the hand.

CHAPTER TEN

Detentions

They were many. For all the state-of-the-art medical facilities Puerto Vallarta counts on these days, there is still no place we can send the mentally ill. They roam the streets until they're picked up by the police and locked behind bars. If you can get them calmed down enough to talk to you, they sometimes make sense. That's when you begin to wonder who the crazy one is. Most of them haven't committed a criminal act, but it's deemed an act of indecency to run around town buck-naked, and that's what many of them seem to want to do. Don't ask me. I am not the psychiatrist. While I was working as the consular agent I saw more nudity than I care to remember.

Chief of Police Salazar, who used to be a judge, called me one day to report the arrest of a nude American man who had tried to climb over the high-security wire fence of the Naval Zone.

Part of my job was to visit any American who was reported to be arrested. This was my very first prison visit. Howard was home, so we went together.

When we got to the jail, the desk sergeant told us, "This one is really wild. They brought him in naked. We don't know who he is and he's speaking some language we don't understand. The only thing we've been able to get out of him is, "*Embajada Americana* seestah," and we don't know what that means. Maybe you'd better go up to see him, Señor. He's wild and he has no clothes on."

I only felt a tiny twinge of guilt for shrinking back and allowing Howard to do what I was supposed to do, but I wasn't looking forward to seeing a crazy man, not even a nude one.

After a few minutes, the sergeant and Howard came back down the stairs. Howard shook his head from side to side and muttered, "Whew! That's a nightmare up there! I don't think he's an American, but I think what he's saying is, 'American Embassy, sister'. Maybe he has a sister working at the Embassy."

"We'll go to the office and make some phone calls. I'll be back as soon as I know something," I told the sergeant

There was a time when people actually answered phones with their own voice. You didn't listen to a long recording, waiting to hear what number to punch in to get to the department you needed.

I told the man in American Citizens Services what I was up against. "I know there probably isn't a chance in hell there's a connection here, but I don't have any other place to go. What can we do?" I asked.

"Jeeze! We get our share of them down here, don't we? Let me check around and see what I can find out. I'll get back to you," he promised.

In less than an hour a woman called me from Mexico City. She identified herself as the wife of one of our consuls and in a soft, hesitant voice asked, "Can you describe the man who is in jail over there?"

I didn't lie to her. I told her I hadn't actually seen him, but my husband had described him as: slender build, dark hair, dark eyes, tan skin, five feet, seven or eight inches, maybe in his mid twenties. I said, "We're not sure he is an American. He's not speaking English, but maybe a mixture of English and Spanish. We thought he might be trying to tell us he has a sister working at the Embassy."

I could hear the despair in her voice when she answered, "That sounds like my brother Sammy. He's been visiting us and was supposed to be on his way back to Estonia. That's where we're from. I don't know what happened. He was supposed to take a flight out of here this morning for New York, but he hasn't been acting normal. He's manic depressive. He's multi-lingual, but when he's in a manic stage, he only speaks our mother tongue and mixes up his other languages. He speaks English."

"We haven't found any identification or luggage yet. It may not be your brother. Give me a little more time. What is your phone number at home?" I promised to call her as soon as we could make positive identification.

My next call was to the Naval Zone to see if this would-be intruder had a suitcase with him when he was caught. Chief of Staff, Captain Maldonado told me his men had found a backpack on the beach near the fence, which he had tried to scale.

"Do you have the backpack with you?" I asked him.

"It's in my office," he replied.

"Would you please check it out and see if there is a passport in it?"

"He's not an American, *Señora*. You don't have to worry about this one. He's Estonian."

With a sinking feeling in my stomach, I asked, "What's his first name?

"Samuel," he replied.

"He may not be an American, but he is kin to one of our consuls at the Embassy. If I come out there, will you give me the backpack?"

"Sure, I'll be waiting for you," he assured me.

After I examined the contents of Sammy's bag, there was no doubt as to who he was, so I called Mrs. Consul in Mexico City. She asked me to get a doctor in to see him while she investigated making arrangements for him to be admitted to a mental facility in Houston.

"Please make sure he gets something to eat," she pleaded.

I didn't tell her the only thing he had eaten so far was his own excrement.

I had no idea how to go about setting up a medical evacuation of this sort. I called over to the Consulate and spoke with my special friend, Jose Luis Palacios, who had worked there for many years and knew all the ropes. He asked if I knew any of the local doctors I could trust with this job.

I immediately thought of Dr. Jose Romo. First of all, he spoke perfect English and I had already contacted him after I had spoken with Sammy's sister. She had suggested a doctor be called in to see him and get him started back on lithium, the medicine of choice for emotional problems in those days. The doctor had mixed and administered what came to be known as The Romo Cocktail.

He was agreeable to escorting Sammy out of the country, but he felt uneasy about going alone. Sammy didn't like those injections and fought every one of them. Dr. Jose didn't think he could give him one strong enough to last all the way to Houston so he asked if his friend, Dr. Fernando Penalva, the dentist, could go along. Whew! That would mean double the price for the sister, but I could certainly understand how Dr. Jose felt and we had to get Sammy out of Mexico, so I called the sister again. She agreed that both doctors should go.

And then there was Decia. Decia was a very pretty woman of about forty years of age. I later learned she had been married and had two children somewhere out West. One day a man living in Yelapa came to the office to talk with me. He had a bizarre story about this American woman who had come to town with a younger American girl, and they had rented a house in Yelapa.

His concern was that there was a steady stream of young Mexican men going in and out of the house all day and night. He said he was not terribly worried about the older woman, but he was for the young girl and he was afraid the Mexican boys might "catch something".

I asked him if he could persuade the Yelapa officials to get the young one on a tourist boat coming back into Puerto Vallarta and radio our port officials to advise me when she arrived at our docks. He did.

From this day on Javier became known as Our Man in Yelapa.

The Yelapa authorities went to the women's house just before the afternoon tourist boat was leaving, rescued the younger one and escorted her to the boat. The story is that Decia came running out of the house, clad in nothing but hot pink leotards and a full length, white mouton coat, waving a dildo at the departing group, yelling "She's mine! She's mine!"

A young man from New York was visiting his father who lived in Puerto Vallarta and he befriended the girl. I think she must have divulged part of the story to him on the boat because when she told him she was going to the Consular Agency, he offered to share a taxi with her. His father lived nearby.

Karen's story was even more off-the-wall. Her mother and father were divorced. Mother lived in California. Father lived in Copenhagen. She had been on her way to visit her father. There was a plane delay in Los Angeles. She became acquainted with Decia in the airport departure lounge. Decia invited Karen to join her for a drink in one of the restaurants nearby. She claims the next thing she knew was she was in Puerto Vallarta. She believed Decia had slipped her a mickey in the cocktail lounge and used what cash she had in her handbag to buy a ticket to Puerto Vallarta.

She arrived in Puerto Vallarta in a confused state and, not even being sure where she was, went blindly along when Decia rented a taxi and she heard her tell the driver, "Boca de Tomatlan." Once at La Boca, Decia hired a *panga* and told the boatman to take them to Yelapa.

Karen claimed the rapid pounding of the boat hitting the waves on the ride to Yelapa cleared the rest of the cobwebs from her mind. She remembered meeting the woman in the boat with her at the airport, but she didn't know how she had gotten wherever she was. She said she began to protest to Decia who told her, "Chill out, kid. We're going to have some fun!"

Karen was a tall, well-proportioned girl with long red hair. She was twenty years old, but looked much older, possibly due to her week-long traumatic ordeal in the jungle village. I've often wondered why she couldn't have found a way to escape before she was rescued. Maybe she really did 'chill out', I don't know.

She was close to becoming hysterical as she sat by my desk that afternoon recounting what she had gone through. Finally, she calmed down enough for us to make a telephone call to her mother.

Not knowing what kind of situation I might be faced with when mother and daughter conversed, I asked if we could have the speaker phone turned on. She agreed and I placed the call. She tearfully told her mother of her harrowing experience and how the boys and Decia had been abusing her daily. I expected the mother to go into a rage or collapse into a sobbing mess, hundreds of miles from her daughter. But no, she didn't. She very calmly said, "Don't worry about it, honey. I can't even give it away these days."

I then spoke with the mother and we made arrangements for her daughter to spend the night in Puerto Vallarta to fly back to Los Angeles the next day.

Within a few days Decia was brought into Puerto Vallarta and Chief Salazar called to advise me of her detention. It was seldom that a female was jailed in Puerto Vallarta, but when there was a mentally disturbed person on the loose, there was no other place to put them.

I never saw the entire cell where women were held, but it had a cot, toilet and washbasin. When I would visit her, she would crawl to the bars, pull herself up to a standing position and struggle to talk to me. I could never make much sense of what she said except she could tell me her name was Decia. She had clothes with her in the cell, but she wouldn't bathe and her hair was a tangled mass of short curls. I took her soap, shampoo, toothbrush and a comb, and tried to encourage her to clean herself up a bit, but she didn't care how she looked.

We had no clue as to her identity.

Finally, one day her son called. He had been looking for her and because she had done a drop-out in Mexico before, he had a hunch she had done it again. I asked Our Man in Yelapa to pack the clothes she had left in the rented house and send them to me.

I don't know how much of this story is true, because I never saw the dildo, but I did see the pink leotards and the full-length, white mouton coat and I did see the unused airline ticket from Los Angeles to Copenhagen and I did hear what the mother told her daughter.

Once again, dear doctors, you came to the rescue. The now famous Romo Cocktail was administered and Dr. Jose and Dr. Fernando were on their way to San Francisco with Decia in tow.

You need to know that when I say, Jail, I mean held under arrest. There were holding cells in the basement of City Hall. This is usually where the town drunks and the *marijuaneros* or other misdemeanors are held for the night. If the infraction is not too serious, the arrestee can pay a fine for his release. That is if he has money.

Sometimes they are even held in hospitals under police guard if they are injured or ill.

These holding cells are called *separos*. If the chief of police deems it fitting, he'll turn the case over to the district attorney and that person is then transferred to what we called the Big Jail.

We sometimes called it Hotel Salazar, Hotel Valenzuela, Hotel Bravo or Hotel Niño, depending on who happened to be the Chief of Police.

The Big Jail was not that enormous prison compound out on the highway toward Ixtapa. Back then it was located across the highway from the Sheraton Hotel in the direction of Red Cross Hospital. Perhaps even you might have been a guest in that hotel at sometime. If you were, I hope you never got to know *La Lobera*. That's what the police called solitary confinement and you've never seen anything in the movies that compares with it. It was a cell located in the basement. That was all there was. No running water, no cot, nothing but a plastic bucket over in a corner.

I saw it one time and the stench has stayed in my memory ever since.

A young man from the Dominican Republic had been arrested for raping a Canadian girl. I should have done what Pat Flanery did when she was helping me one day. Another man from the Dominican Republic had also been arrested. She took the call from the police department and went to the *separos* to visit the prisoner. When she discovered his nationality, she said, "Nope, Chief, he ain't one of ours."

I got caught on this one because his mama worked in New York, legally or not, I don't know. He asked me to phone her and let her know where he was.

He was in for an extended period before he was finally deported. In the meantime, his worried mother would call me from time to time. She sent money to me to give to him. When I went to make the delivery, he was in *La Lobera.* I never asked what he had done that was so bad he was punished with that hell hole.

Bruce was another mental case who went behind the bars. He, his eight-month-pregnant girlfriend and one of our local doctors decided to swim nude at midnight on Conchas Chinas Beach, a bit south of town. The police didn't think that was proper behavior, so they arrested the group.

The smart-crazy doctor was able to talk his way into a phone call to his Father Doctor in Guadalajara, who came for him immediately. The other two were not so lucky.

When I visited them in jail, both had recovered their clothes, but Bruce had definitely not recovered his emotional stability. He claimed they came from Heaven, his name was David and Mary would soon be giving birth to Jesus Christ.

I never found out much about Mary's background. She was Caucasian, she was very obviously pregnant and David's name was Bruce.

According to Mary, Bruce and David were brothers. One day they went for a ride on their motorbikes. David's bike flipped him over an embankment, killing him instantly. Bruce believed it was he who had died, and his soul entered David's body on the spot. From then on, he called himself David.

My report was made on Bruce. Mary provided me with her mother's phone number and I called her to get financial help in getting these people transferred to a mental facility in Guadalajara in preparation for their repatriation home.

Bruce was placed in Red Cross Hospital with a police guard. Mary was free to sit by his side or to go to a cheap hotel. She chose the hotel.

I spent most of the morning making arrangements for Bruce's admittance to the hospital in Guadalajara. I decided to take a look in on him late in the afternoon. I packed sandwiches in case he or Mary would eat. I opened the door to his room and saw that he had been bound, spread-eagled, to the bed with sheets. He was a small, skinny, dark skinned man who looked as if he had no strength whatsoever. Wrong. When he saw me, he rose up off the bed and began yelling, "Death! Death! Death!" I quickly backed out of the room and drove back home, badly shaken.

Lieutenant Mario Salas Bernal was my nighttime body guard in those days. There was nothing official about this arrangement other than Admiral Tomas Ortega Beltran declared it was to be this way.

Howard was working in Houston and came home on weekends, but emergencies had a way of arising during the week, many times at night, and not only on weekends. Admiral Ortega had laid the word down that I was never to go out of the house on one of those nighttime mercy missions without an escort.

I suppose Admiral Ortega thought I would be safe enough to walk out of my house, down to my garage and drive to the center of town to pick Lieutenant Mario up in front of his apartment.

He would be suited up in dress khakis and carrying a little bag like the ones banks used to give to their best customers. I learned that those bags were the gentleman body guard's version of a holster for his gun. When you think about this as a security measure, it was not the most sophisticated body guard service, but it was comforting to have a strong, big shouldered, masculine hunk in uniform with me on those night ramblings through the streets.

Tonight Lieutenant Mario and I were on our way to Red Cross Hospital. We found Bruce lying on the floor with his arms handcuffed behind his back. Both legs were bandaged. The nurses and paramedics stood to one side while the policeman guarding Bruce explained to me how Bruce had become extremely agitated, broken his bonds from the bed, broke the iron bed into pieces with his bare hands, taken one of those pieces, stabbed himself in both thighs and ran out of the hospital into an open field nearby.

With much gentle care, he was brought back into the hospital and his wounds were attended.

Give me a break, fellows. I'm not blonde, blue eyed, don't have dimples nor am I pigeon-toed. I asked to make a phone call. Again, Dr. Jose Romo was aroused from his good night's sleep to help me.

Bruce was still lying on the floor and heavily sedated when Dr. Romo arrived. He knelt by Bruce's side and removed the bandages from his self-inflicted wounds. He fell back in astonishment.

"This is gun powder around these wounds!"

We learned later Bruce had indeed broken his bonds from the bed and run out into the open field near the hospital. The police guard had managed to catch up with him and shot him through both thighs, so he would run no more that night.

The next day found Pat Flanery and me sitting in my car under a tree outside of Red Cross Hospital engaged in a stare-down confrontation with Chief of Police Salazar and his deputy, Miguel Angel Villanueva. There were two trees in the parking area. They had their tree, and we had ours. I still don't know how news travels in the jungle, but they knew we were preparing for Operation Bruce at that hour and they arrived at the scene about the time we did.

The Chief, AKA Judge, and his deputy got out of the official *Departmento de Seguridad Publico* Volkswagen and walked over to our tree.

Pat and I made no move to get out of my car to greet them. The Chief came to my side of the car, peered into the window and said, "*Señora,* I want you to know that was not gun powder around the wounds on his legs."

In the most lady-like, gentile, diplomatic words I could come up with at that time, I replied, "Please step aside, Chief." But in my mind, the words were a bit stronger. "A'm taking this guy outta here and dontya try to stop me!"

I truly don't think Salazar understood Suthrun Spanish too well, but he did back off and retreated to his VW.

Pat and I sat there waiting for our transport vehicle to arrive. Mind you, we had no ambulances in those times, which could transport a patient out of Puerto Vallarta. Lieutenant Mario's friend Marco, the son of Mr. Villegas, of mortician fame, arrived in his father's new funeral hearse. He was to be the driver.

Pregnant Mary was there, a paramedic was ready to accompany them, but the effects of the calming medication Dr. Romo had administered were wearing off and they were facing a five hour drive to the nearest mental hospital in Guadalajara.

Marco and the paramedic put their heads together and engaged in what appeared to be anxious conversation.

Marco said to me, "*Señora,* we are worried that he may become too wild while we are on the road. Do you think you can get us some handcuffs?"

"I don't know, but I'll certainly give it a try." By this time the chief of police and his deputy had driven away and I wouldn't have wanted to ask them for a favor on this particular day anyway. However, I did ask the police guard who had been ordered to stay by our side until the ambulance/hearse left. No way was he going to turn loose of any piece of official gear and I can't say that I blamed him. What do I do now?

We didn't have cell phones in those days, so I went back inside the Red Cross Hospital and called Admiral Ortega, explained our predicament and asked him if he might happen to have some handcuffs we could borrow.

"They will be delivered to you in exactly eleven minutes," he promised, and they were there in eleven minutes. Not ten. Not twelve, but eleven. Pat and I heaved a sigh of relieve as we watched the black hearse pull away from the hospital.

The following day an article appeared in a Guadalajara newspaper, which read:

"BLACK AMERICAN MAN ARRIVES AT HOSPITAL, SHOT AT CLOSE RANGE THROUGH BOTH LEGS."

It appears that the paper got it right this time.

Mary Helen was another one of our colorful visitors. She and her boyfriend, Mark, had come down from San Antonio to work in the time-share business. I've told you about that before!

After a few weeks, Mary Helen decided she had rather mix cement. There was a policeman who worked as desk sergeant in the separos. He loved to talk like Donald Duck. I soon learned to understand him or most of the time I did. He was a likeable guy, but a strange looking Mexican. First of all, he had red hair, he was tall and he had a very pock-marked light complexion. The Puerto Vallarta sun had made his skin look as if he had leprosy and I had to overcome a repulsion just to shake hands with him, but we got along well together. When he quacked into the phone, I knew trouble was brewing.

He told me a construction worker had reported an American woman hanging around their construction site. The worker told him he didn't believe she had a place to sleep and he feared for her safety if she decided to spend the night there. He also told Officer Donald Duck that he thought she might be "un poco loco".

I told the Duck, "There's nothing I can do about it at this point, but call me if you bring her in and I'll see what we can do."

The police and I were beginning to develop a routine about these things. Not all, but most of the arrests were made at night. The police had my home phone number and would call me early in the morning before I left the house to go to the office if there had been an American arrested during the night. I would usually scramble an extra egg, make a sandwich, toss in a piece of fruit and set off to make my first prison visit of the day with Care Package in hand. Prison rations were slim at any time, but non-existent in the *separos*.

The phone rang. It was Sergeant Duck. "She's here, *Señora* and she doesn't have any clothes on."

"Is she little or big and fat" I asked

"I would say, umh, about the size of our secretary, Lupe," he replied.

"O.K. I'll be there soon," I told him.

Another thing you are never told in the training courses nor is it ever mentioned in the famous tomes of Foreign Affairs Manuals is your need to have a stash of used clothing on hand. I kept men, women and children's clothes in my home and also stored at the office. My friends' cast-offs truly came in handy at times.

So Care Package and approximately a size twelve dress in hand, I walked down the hill and into town to see who Hotel Villanueva's newest American guest might be.

She was sitting very calmly on a stool inside one of the holding cells smoking a cigarette. Cops won't buy you food, but you can usually bum a cigarette off them. I could have been envious of her good-looking naked body, but it was splashed all over in grey cement She had told the police her name was Mary Helen.

I said to her, "Mary Helen, I've brought you something to eat and some clothes for you to put on. Let's talk and see if we can find a way to get you out of this mess. Tell me a bit about yourself and where you live?"

According to Mary Helen, she had been "married to a true son-of-a bitch doctor up in San Antonio. He is screwing around with other women and so I just decided to come down here with Mark. I got a little tired of that time-share shit, so I decided to do something else."

"And what was it you decided to do?" I asked her.

"Help those poor Mexicans mix cement. They don't know how to go about doing it."

"And you do?"

"Well, I certainly know how to have fun doing it. You put that cement and cal in that wooden tub they use to mix in and then you pour some water in. Then you climb in and pretend you're stomping grapes like they do in Italy when they're making wine. You simply jump up and down."

I nodded my head in agreement and said, "That does sound like fun, but tell me, Mary Helen, why did you take all your clothes off?"

"Because I didn't want to get cement all over them."

Crazy-smart or smart-crazy?

In our friendly chat, I learned the name and phone number of her son-of-a-bitch husband. I also learned where she and Mark had been staying. I left her to eat the sandwich and made my way to the office and a phone.

Dr. So-And-So was not so bad after all. He pre-paid an airline ticket for her to return to San Antonio and promised to have someone meet her at the airport. Mary Helen was to spend one more night in jail.

I located Mark and brought him up to date on what had happened to his girlfriend. He said he wanted nothing more to do with her; she was crazy and he was glad to be rid of her. He offered to pack her things if I wanted to come pick them up. We agreed that I would come to his waterfront condo the following morning before he went to his time-share job.

At eight o'clock I was knocking on his door. He invited me in and closed the door behind us. Short, bulging belly, hawk-nosed, black hair greased and molded into something of a pompadour, smartly dressed and wearing what looked like gold Rolex watch. I couldn't blame Mary Helen for mixing cement.

Mark handed me her handbag, which fortunately, contained her passport and tourist visa. He pointed to a suitcase on the floor and said, "That's hers. You know, Mrs. McGill, I'm really worried. I'm afraid that all these problems I've had with Mary Helen is going to make me impotent."

"Unh unh," I thought with a rapidly pounding heart, "McGill, you have done it again. Nobody, but nobody knows where I am this morning and here I stand in this condo with a sick man who is worried about his sex life." Acting as calmly as I could, I picked up the suitcase and handbag, and said to him, "Mark, back in San Antonio, there are professionals who can help you. If you don't know anyone, I suggest you start out with the Yellow Pages and look under C for Counseling. If you don't find what you're looking for, try Therapist, look for Sex Therapist."

I left the room, made a fast retreat to the safety of my car in the parking lot and let out a big sigh of relief. "Don't you ever get yourself in that situation again," I told myself.

Another one of my cases was Robbie, who was a long way from home. He had come down from Philadelphia to rent one of those water scooters and enjoy a solo tour of Bahia de Banderas.

This is the biggest bay in Mexico. It's on the Pacific Ocean, but the waters are not necessarily tranquil. Navy folks have told me the bottom of the ocean is similar to the topography of the area. Puerto Vallarta is located on the coast, but the mountains run down to meet the sandy beach and they continue on out into the ocean. It's very difficult to anchor boats in the uneven bay with choppy waters.

The scooter ran out of gas and, eventually, it and Robbie were washed ashore onto a rocky area south of town. He escaped uninjured, but the scooter was smashed on the rocks. Naturally, Robbie didn't bring enough money with him to pay for the damage to the scooter, so he was arrested. This case was turned over to the district attorney before I was advised, so I interviewed him in another part of City Hall, not in the basement where the *separos* were located.

So many of these cases are truly sickening to see. Robbie was a young man of twenty-two years. He had dark hair and extremely fair skin, except for his red nose. He had caught a cold after his surprise swim in the ocean and he kept wiping his runny nose on the palm of his hand. He didn't wipe like some people do with one finger wiping from side to side. He put his nose in this hand and wiped straight up like I've seen little kids do.

Robbie could never tell me where he left his suitcase or if he had even ever checked into a hotel. He had no identification, but he did tell me his name and where he was from. He could remember his father's phone number and asked that I call him. I left him a package of Kleenex and headed back to the office.

Robbie's father was not happy to hear of his son's imprisonment and now as I look back on this case, I suspect he'd been through this before. I asked him if his son had shown any signs of emotional instability before, and he answered, "Ever since he was a teen-ager."

I could probably spring Robbie if he would send money to cover damage to the scooter and an airline ticket. He told me that he didn't have that kind of money and Robbie would just have to stay where he was. He stayed behind bars for about three months.

From time to time, one of the consular officials would come from Guadalajara to check over cases and do some glad-handing around City Hall.

That glad-handing bit is very important. We may not like that politician, but we have to work with him, and the job is much easier if it's done in a friendly atmosphere.

Julio Arias, the Consul General in Guadalajara came to town and after we did our glad-handing, we made a prison visit. Consul Arias bought Robbie a soda from the vending machine in the outer office of the Big Jail, pulled up a chair and began to talk to him; he on one side of the bars, Robbie on the other. Robbie asked Consul Arias if he could speak with him without my hearing. I nodded and gladly backed away to wait outside the door.

When Consul Arias left the prison and we were on our way back into town, I asked him, "What did Robbie have to say he didn't want me to hear?"

"He was complaining that he's not sleeping because the other prisoners won't keep their hands off him." I was very innocent in those days about what took place inside over-crowded prisons.

Consul Arias said, "What's happening to this boy is inhumane. We are going to have to do something about it."

I don't know how this was managed. The United States Government doesn't pick up the tab for American citizens to be repatriated. There is a method whereby the person in need can request a loan of monies for repatriation. If that person, for any reason, can't sign the solicitation and the document promising to repay the loan, some other responsible person must do it for him. The judge was more than willing to release Robbie, but he had no place to go. Consul Arias telephoned somebody in Washington, D.C. at the State Department and that somebody called Robbie's father in Philadelphia. Somehow arrangements were made.

I received a call from Guadalajara, "Robbie is on his way out. See if you can find a medical escort for him to Houston. Another department will take over there and escort him on to Philadelphia."

The rest was easy. I called my wonderful old friend, Jack Wilhoit. "Hey, Jack, you know that boy I've been telling you about? The one who is in jail? Well, he has been pardoned and we are going to do a medical escort out, but he doesn't have any clothes for travel. What do you have in your closet you can afford to give me? It's cold weather up north and he is going all the way to Philadelphia."

Then I called Dr. Jose. "Doc, how much will you charge to do a medical escort service to Houston, apart from air transportation, hotel and meals?"

We settled on a price and plans were made to travel on a Friday afternoon. I also decided to go to Houston for the weekend.

Jack brought me a pair of grey flannels, a shirt, warm sweater, clean underwear and socks. I left the office at closing time, armed with prison release form, immigration documents, clean clothes, and a bar of soap and headed for the jail.

Dr. Jose would pick up Robbie at the jail; take him to the airport and board with him prior to other passengers boarding. We had worked this all out with the airline the day before and we had decided it would be best if I didn't sit near them on the plane.

We made a stop in Mazatlan for passengers to be processed through Immigration, but this also had been planned ahead of time. Dr. Jose, Robbie, and I would stay on the plane and immigration officials would check our papers without us having to deplane.

All seemed to be going well. We were on our way flying into Houston. There had been no ruckus coming from where Dr. Jose and Robbie were seated.

I decided to take a stroll down the aisle and see what was happening. Dr. Jose saw me coming and rolled his eyes back into his head. "How is it going, Doc?" I whispered as I turned my face away from the row where they were seated. Robbie was jabber-jabbering non-stop and staring out the window. Exasperated, Dr. Jose said, "He's driving me crazy. He won't shut up."

I sympathized with him, "We'll soon be there." As I walked away, I heard the doctor say, "Dammit, Robbie, I'm telling you for the last time! Put your bird back in your pants!"

Howard met our plane in Houston, along with two employees from the Health and Human Services Department of Texas, who were supposed to take over the escort. After assessing the situation, the HHS reps decided it would be to their benefit to convince Dr. Romo to carry on with the escort service.

There was about a two hour wait before Robbie's plane was due to take off. We decided to wait with them. I knew Dr. Jose needed a break from his escort duty, so I suggested he leave Robbie with us seated in the departures lounge while he went to one of the fast food restaurants in the area for a cup of coffee. He thought that was a superb idea, but he cried out, "What if he takes his bird out?"

We thought we could handle Robbie's bird and sent Dr. Jose off to his much deserved break. Twenty five years have passed since that day and we still refer to Dr. Jose as The Bird Doctor. He refers to Howard as The Bird Man.

The Big Jail, near the Red Cross Hospital, was built on three levels. The ladies' cells were upstairs and off to one side of a corridor. This gave the women some privacy.

The men's cells were also on the upper level, but around a corner from the ladies' cells. There was an open air area in front of these cells. Although the men were not allowed outside, it did provide for some light and air circulation. These were what we called tanks, not individual cells. They were built to hold approximately twenty men, but many times there were as many as forty hot, stinking, sweating mean bodies in one tank.

Most of the time a foreigner was held in a smaller separate cell if conditions were not too over-crowded. Prisoners held in this area were not expected to be in for an extended period of time. They were either waiting to be sentenced or hoping for a bail bond to be set they could afford to pay. Once it was determined they were not leaving anytime soon, they were transferred to a larger area on the ground floor.

From the street you entered a small cubby-hole, which contained a desk, a chair, an ice box, and a fat bellied sergeant who wore several gold chains around his neck and gold bracelets on both arms, not to mention the gold rings on almost every finger except his thumbs. He even had gold fillings in his front teeth!

After I got over my initial fear of going out to the place, Sarge and I became buddies. Sink or swim, you know. Off to one side of this entrance was the Director's office, which was a joke.

Valentino was the only director I ever knew out there who even kept records. He invited me into his office one day, and like a kid with a new toy, showed me his sophisticated method of keeping records. He actually had bought large index cards and had written the name of each prisoner on a card. He had a new Polaroid camera, which he was mighty proud of also, so he snapped mug shots of the prisoner and pasted them on his card.

He wrote down as much information about the prisoner as he could, including the date he was arrested and for what reason. He told me, "I'm thinking about getting me one of those little ink pads and making their finger prints."

The main action took place on the other side of Sarge's desk. When I interviewed a prisoner, he was called up to the barred door; an armed guard stood by my side while the prisoner and I talked through the bars.

I could see an open courtyard behind him and other prisoners were milling around. Although I never saw beyond that courtyard, the prisoners on this level were always clean and wore fresh clothes. They were responsible for their own laundry and meals. Rations were provided by City Administration, but the meal preparation was up to them. They always had plenty of beans, rice and tortillas. They never had beef or pork.

Chief Villanueva told me, "We give them fish. Never give them red meat. It makes them too mean."

The fish that was delivered to the jail were leftovers after you bought your filet from the boat or the market. The fish carcass, including the head, was tossed into a pot of water along with a few veggies plus spices and you soon had a nourishing Bouillabaisse.

They ate fruit, eggs, toast or tortillas and beans for breakfast. Many of the prisoners' families brought them meals every day. If they had money, they could send out for food. I'm not talking about Domino's pizza or take-out Chinese because they didn't exist down here back then. However, there was a fast food shack across the street from the jail that made a fairly tasty hamburger. Do you want to know how I know so much about prison rations? It's because I "played football" for about six months with a couple of 49ers.

The story about Tyrone X and Leroy XX, the 49ers, got my attention. They were already in the Big Jail on the ground floor before I was aware of their arrest and went for my first visit with them.

They were big enough to be 49ers, but badly out of shape. Their story, if true, was that they had made a drug drop for a Mr. Harris up in California. Mr. Harris had promised them $5,000 dollars each when the job was completed. When they went to Mr. Harris to collect, he told them he could only give them each $2,000 dollars in cash, but he offered them his American Express credit card and told them they could charge up to $6,000 dollars on anything they wanted. They decided to visit beautiful, sunny, tropical Puerto Vallarta.

· They checked into one of the hotels located in the Marina and registered with Mr. Harris' credit card. They had a wonderful time for about three weeks.

They made good friends with the hotel manager, whom we later learned was in on the scam. He even advanced cash to them on Mr. Harris' credit card. They wined and dined in the finest of Puerto Vallarta's bars and restaurants.

Frequently, they invited the hotel manager to join them for an evening on the town. The inevitable had to happen and one night it did. They had run up a sizeable tab in a nightclub. The time came to pay the bill and Leroy offered the credit card. The card was rejected because Mr. Harris had reported it stolen.

None of them had enough cash to cover the bill, so the nightclub manager called the cops.

All three men were arrested, but the hotel manager was released the following day. By this time, Leroy and Tyrone had mounted a bill at the hotel, which rose into thousands of dollars, and not a chance in sight of paying it. The hotel manager was bound by duty, and the fear of losing his job, to press charges against them. It looked like they would be guests of Hotel Bravo for a good spell.

I introduced myself to them and told them I had come to take some personal information from them. I filled out my prison report; complete with their names, dates of birth, addresses back in USA and next of kin.

The one called Leroy asked me, "Lady, what part of the United States do you come from?"

"Mississippi," I replied.

Leroy turned to Tyrone and said, "Aw, shit, Bubba, we in a heapa trouble."

"No doubt about that, boys," I countered, "but that's not my fault and it doesn't have anything to do with where I'm from either."

Tyrone was married, but he was on the outs with his wife and didn't want her to know anything about him. Neither of them wanted their families to be contacted.

Both had told me early in the interview they played football for the 49'ers. I asked them, "If you play for the 49'ers, don't you think some of your team members, coach or even Mr. DiBartolo could gather the money together to pay your debt and you could get out of here?"

"No, no! We don't want Mr. Ed or nobody else to know we're in here." Tyrone exclaimed.

"Fine with me," I told them, "I won't contact anybody." I advised them that I had no idea if they would be transferred to a bigger prison in Guadalajara or not, but that I would visit them from time to time to check on them as long as they were held in Puerto Vallarta.

Prison visits were ordinarily made about every two weeks unless a problem arose. One day Sarge telephoned and said, "*Señora*, your boys want to see you." After ascertaining that they were all right, I told him, "O.K. Tell them I'll be out tomorrow afternoon."

It was one of those sweltering hot, humid summer days. It was even steamier inside the prison walls, and the open air patio didn't offer much relief for the prisoners.

They were complaining about the food they were receiving and I couldn't blame them, but I didn't hire on as a galley cook. There is such a thing as a Dietary Supplement Loan provided by the State Department, but I had my doubts that these two blubbery fat boys would qualify.

The dietary supplement is usually used when the food is absolutely inedible and a prisoner's health is endangered. Here, this was not the case.

I agreed with them that the food probably was boring and tasteless, but there was nothing I could do about it. I tried to encourage them by telling them they should loose some weight and the food was nourishing, if unappetizing.

Tyrone asked me if I would buy him a pair of shorts. "You know? The kind that has a matching shirt and little boats sailing around on them?" I was reminded of that old adage: Beggars can't be choosers. But I did feel sorry for them in that terrible heat, so I went to my fattest friends. I managed to collect two pairs of shorts for each of them plus some light weight shirts.

A week or so passed and Sarge called me. "*Señora*, your boys had to go to the hospital last night to get their heads sewed up."

"Heads sewed up? Whatever for? What happened?" I asked him.

"They broke into the dispensary. They stuck their thumbs in all the eggs and drank them down! Sucked down the entire week's supply!"

"Dogs! Just like dogs!" I thought. Sarge assured me their wounds had been properly treated at Regional Hospital, but I decided to look in on them myself.

Rafael, my daytime guard, and I went to the prison and they had, indeed, had their heads sewn up the night before. The other prisoners were so angry that they had been deprived of their breakfast eggs for the week they jumped on Tyrone and Leroy and opened good-sized gashes on their heads with their bare knuckles.

Tyrone and Leroy said they had had worse injuries on the football field. I was surprised to see them both dressed in long pants and not in the shorts I had sent to them. Curious about this, I asked, "Why aren't you wearing the shorts I sent you?"

Leroy, almost in an apologetic and embarrassed voice, said, "Jenny, you don't know about us men folks. We can't wear those short shorts without somethin' under them."

Oops! I had heard about such things but I had forgotten.

They were still complaining about their food. I said to them, "Why don't you let me call some family member or a friend for you? Maybe they could send you money and you could order a hamburger or a ham and cheese sandwich from across the street to change the routine a bit?" They finally agreed to sign a Privacy Act Waiver form allowing me to contact one of the parents on their behalf.

A woman answered the telephone at Leroy's father's house. I asked to speak to Mr. XX. When I explained to him who I was and why I was calling, he said, "I told them boys the law was gonna ketch up with 'em one of these days and it look like it sure did."

He said he might be able to send a little amount of money and that he would talk with Leroy's brother to see if he could send some more. I told him I had suggested to both, Leroy and Tyrone, when they were first arrested, that they might want to contact some of their 49'er teammates or the coach to request some aid.

"Teammates?" he cried. "They don't work for the 49'ers! They don't work for nobody! I works for the 49'ers! I'm a lineman!"

I know very little about football and have no interest in learning, but I'm thinking, "Lineman? Leroy is thirty-two years old. His father could have sired him as young as fifteen, but more likely around twenty. At best calculation, father's age would probably fall between forty-seven and fifty-two. That seemed a bit old to me to be playing professional football. I questioned him, "Lineman? You are a lineman for the 49'ers?"

"Yes maam! I marks the chalk lines on the field!"

I reported each of my prison visits to my supervisory post in Guadalajara. We had a different Consul General by now. Richard Morefield had been held hostage four-hundred-forty-four days in our Embassy in Iran and he had known hunger. He took pity on our egg-sucking boys and directed me to get the proper forms filled out and signed by them to see if we could get a Dietary Supplement Loan.

I typed up the forms and sent Rafael to the jail for their signatures. He returned, walked into the office where I was typing up, yet, another one of those (& %$%&/()) government forms. One of the young consuls had advised me, when I first went to work, "We try not to drown in paperwork, but it is better to Cover Your Ass in paperwork rather than be caught not remembering what you did." In dip jargon, we call that CYA-ing. So there I sat, CMyA-ing when Rafael walked in asked me, "*Señora*, what means, "Fuck you?"

My typing hands stopped in mid-air, blood rushed to my face and my eyes almost popped from their sockets, "Where did you hear that word?"

"The boys." He handed me the unsigned forms and a page torn from a magazine. The page bore a sketch of the country of Africa. Someone had penciled in on the margin of the page, "Fuck you!"

I kept a file in the bottom drawer of my desk, which I called the Blue Funk File. Sometimes I would get a nice "thank you" note from somebody I had helped or someone might send me a funny greeting card. When I had an especially rough day, I could usually lighten my blue funk with something I had stored in that file.

One of my naughty, nasty, mean friends had sent me just the card I wanted now. On the front of the card was a humongously fat woman, with dark red lips, shiny coifed hair and big gold loop earrings. She was wearing a bright yellow dress, which set off her walnut colored skin magnificently. The caption under her picture read: I AM WOMAN. Inside the card were only four words. DON'T FUCK WITH ME!

I made several Photostatic copies of this card and, with a colored marker, put different colored dresses on that big woman. Each day for a week or so, Rafael would deliver one of the cards to "the boys" in jail.

I never saw Leroy or Tyrone after that. Chief Bravo heard a rumor that a jail-break was being planned by some of the Mexican prisoners. He had the opportunity to transfer a load of inmates to Puente Grande, the big, Big Prison in Guadalajara and he included "my boys" in the shipment.

Judges have the right to pardon certain cases if they decide to do so. They frequently do this at Christmastime. Christmas was approaching. Leroy and Tyrone had been behind bars for a bit over ten months and it didn't appear that any money would ever be coming to pay their debt. But it was, after all, Christmas. *Voila!* They were pardoned and repatriated back to California. At least, they can cheer for the 49'ers.

Tracy was a breath of fresh air after the 49'ers, although she loved her eggs too.

A fisherman named Alonso came to see me one day. He had lived in the United States for many years, but now had retired to his *querencia* by the sea. Alonso spoke good English and seemed to be a decent man. He told me about Tracy.

She had absolutely destroyed the inside of a schoolroom in Bucerias. It was summertime and classes were not in session. Somebody had left the school door unlocked. She went through the school like a demented dervish, turned every desk upside down, ripped the blackboards off the walls and we won't talk about what she did to the chairs. The police locked her up.

I had a pretty good idea of what to expect. I grabbed an old bed sheet and then called Chief Bravo to tell him I needed to go into the neighboring state and bring a "loquita" prisoner back to Puerto Vallarta. This Chief and I had not bumped heads too hard at this point, so he agreed to hold her until I could find out who she was.

Ordinarily, moving a prisoner from one state to another would take an Act of Congress, but Bucerias police were only too happy to be rid of Tracy. There were two cells in a brick building set across the street from another brick building, which housed the Chief of Police and his three officers.

Howard had gone with me on this trip and one of the deputies walked us over to the holding cell. As we approached, we could hear a girl singing in a loud, happy voice. The deputy looked over at us, shrugged his shoulders, shook his head, turned and walked back to his office on the other side of the street.

We couldn't see anybody in either of the cells when we first entered. It was dark inside. There were no windows and the only light came from the open door. The singing had stopped and there was an eerie quiet about the place. Egg shells were strewn all over the floor of one cell.

Just about the time I decided our prisoner had flown the coop, we were bombarded with a blast of hard-boiled eggs being thrown from somewhere up above.

As we were ducking eggs, the loud singing resumed.

"My stepmother was an aaa-lien! My stepmother was an aaa-lien!"

A wild, slender young beauty with long, tousled blonde hair had climbed up the bars and was swinging from the top one, as in Tarzan and Jane. Jane wore a loin cloth. Tracy didn't.

I thought, "Dear me, we can't take this thing back to Puerto Vallarta in our car like this," so I walked back to the Chief's quarters and asked him if he would send her over with two of his deputies in their truck. "*Con gusto, Señora, con mucho gusto.*" He was more than happy to be of help. He would have a clean jail cell soon.

We wrapped Tracy in a sheet, and she sat between the driver and the escort in the police truck. Howard and I followed and we could see her head bobbing and swinging as she sang all the way from Bucerias to Puerto Vallarta. "My stepmother was an aaa-lien! My stepmother was an aaa-lien!"

She had managed to lose everything she owned except a little blue macramé pouch she wore around her neck. She grabbed onto that pouch when we put her in the police truck in Bucerias. When we put her in the holding cell in Puerto Vallarta, she was still hanging onto it.

While I was probing and trying to draw information out of her, I asked, "What's with that bag around your neck? What's in it?" She clung to it even tighter. I was reminded of a picture I had seen of a terrified doe before the hunter came in for the kill. After a lot of coaxing, she gave me the pouch. In it was her California drivers' license and a scrap of paper with the notation, "Daddy - 510-"

Those guys who work in Department of Public Safety sometimes can be a fountain of information. I don't know how they do it, but they must have genies working for them. In less than two hours, I had a phone number for Tracy's father in Los Angeles.

In the meantime, a young man named Erik came to the office. He said he had met Tracy when she first came to Puerto Vallarta, but lost track of her. One of his friends had seen her in the Bucerias police truck when she was being brought into town. He asked if he could help.

I told him California DPS was trying to locate her father, and he volunteered to accompany her home if necessary.

Tracy's father was expecting my call. I told him, "Mr. Southerland, Tracy is with me in Puerto Vallarta, Mexico."

We made arrangements for him to pre-pay air tickets for Tracy and her friend, Erik, to fly out the following afternoon.

In cases like this, a lot of paperwork has to be done. You have to make sure the airline personnel you'll be working with are fully aware of what is going on. You must have the local Immigration's written permission for the person to leave the country. You have to reasonably satisfy US Immigration that the person coming in is an American citizen or legal resident with rights to return. I'm sure it is much more complicated these days. It should be.

I spent the rest of the afternoon and well over into the evening trying to make the next day go smoothly. I took time out to make a sandwich for Tracy and take her some clothes to wear. This was summertime and it was hot. I scrounged around in my closet and came up with a pair of shorts and a scooped neck t-shirt. She seemed to be comfortable and settled in for the night. She lay curled up on the floor, humming her song, "My stepmother was an alien, an alien, an alien. My stepmother was an alien."

The next morning I scrambled an extra egg for Tracy's sandwich, got dressed and headed out to work.

As I walked down to the garden to meet my guard, I saw our neighbor, Paul Bancroft, going out for his morning walk. I asked him if he had ever been inside a Mexican jail. He hadn't.

"Come go with me! You can tell your poker buddies about it," I invited him.

Paul and his wife Kitty were well-known San Francisco socialites in the seventies. They entertained often and lavishly in Puerto Vallarta also. Kitty watched her guests with the eye of a hawk during cocktail hour. She'd have her seating arrangement made out ahead of time. However, if she saw you talking too long to somebody she had planned for you to sit by during dinner, she would rearrange the seating. She meant you weren't going to run out of something to say to your dinner partner. She used to tell Paul, "When I die, you'll be just another pair of pants around San Francisco."

This morning Mr. Another Pair of Pants was walking with me to jail.

We said "Good morning" to the desk sergeant and he motioned for us to come on through the swinging half door.

We were now in the basement of City Hall where the *separos* are located. There were two banged-up grey metal desks on one side of the swinging door. Lupe, the secretary, sat at one desk typing on her circa 1920 manual typewriter. Sergeant Duck sat behind the other. There was a closed door between these two desks, which led back into the Chief's office where he shares space with his deputy. There was an open doorway to the left of Lupe's desk, which leads into a hallway. The hallway was about four feet wide and ran in front of the four *separos*. There was an open barred window at one end of the hallway. The window was at ceiling level down in the basement, but at street level outside. There was a door at the other end of the hallway, which went out into the parking garage.

I could see Tracy as we came into the hallway. I don't know what happened to the shorts I had taken her. Somebody else had provided her with a blouse. She had stuck her legs through the arm holes of my scooped neck t-shirt and cinched it around her waist with a piece of rope.

In shocked disbelief I exclaimed, "Tracy! What in the world do you have on?" She did a little pivot, turned her back to us and bent over.

There before God and everybody, she mooned us!

Paul got a lot of mileage out of that visit to jail. The last time I saw him, he was still talking about it.

Those same *separos* were temporary home to one of the Ten Most Wanted.

Michael almost escaped before I ever met him. He had been arrested in the parking lot of the Sheraton Hotel. He was surprised early one morning by a hotel security guard going off duty. He was trying to sell some gold jewelry and just a wee bit of cocaine to a hotel guest. He spent one night in the *separos* where he made friends with another prisoner who was to be released the following morning.

Michael had managed to stash a few dollars, which the guards didn't find when he was arrested. He paid his prison buddy about $5.00 dollars to buy him a hack saw blade.

He claimed that true to his word, within about an hour after his new friend's release, there was a metallic clang outside his cell door. The saw blade had been thrown through the high window from the street above. It fell close to the wall of the hallway running in front of the cells and just out of his reach. He pulled off his pants, and holding onto them, reached through the bars and fished the saw blade over to his cell door.

The vertical bars were spaced about eight inches apart and there was one single horizontal bar across the middle of the door. Michael sat down on the floor behind the bars and began to work. It took him about three hours to finish his job without making noise or attracting the attention of the guards.

He told me later that his timing was all wrong on this. His plans were to make his break at three o'clock in the afternoon when there was bustling activity of the change of guard duty. He figured he could be out of his cell, through the door leading into the basement parking garage, up the ramp, out on the streets and lost in the crowds before any of the guards missed him.

Around two-thirty in the afternoon he decided to test the bar and see how much more sawing he had to do. To his surprise and dismay, the bar popped right out when he pressed his foot against it. It was now or never. He had to make a go for it.

He ran though the garage and on to the streets as he'd planned. He actually got further than I would've ever dreamed without him getting shot.

He ran south along the Malecon until he got to the bridge crossing the River Cuale. He ducked down a side street and came to the southwest entrance to the public market. You almost have to know it's there to see it, but there's a swinging bridge cantilevered across the river leading to the island where the tourist shops are located. That's where they caught him. Charging across that bucking bridge at high speed.

The Mexican law reads that no foreigner is required to appear before a judicial authority without an approved qualified translator. These translators are called *perito traductores*. We didn't have any in Puerto Vallarta.

My Canadian counterparts spoke English, Spanish, and French. I spoke English and Spanish. We knew Mexicans who spoke very good English. We knew two or three Germans and Italians, but none of us were *perito traductores*.

This is where one can really be caught in a bind. The Foreign Affairs Manuals of all our countries say consular representatives are not expected to act as translators. As a matter of fact, it is frowned upon. But when the district attorney or a judge calls you up and says, "Come down here and tell me what this guy's saying," what are you going to do? We always act in the best interest of our countrymen, right?

Michael was extraordinarily handsome with the greenest green eyes I've ever seen in my life. I know now they were tinted contact lens. His pretty little blonde wife, Rose, was in the judge's chambers with us. Michael began his story and I translated.

Michael said he and Rose lived with his father in Rowlett, Texas. They had borrowed the father's pick-up truck and driven to Puerto Vallarta. He was trying to trade Rose's gold jewelry for a hit of cocaine. He was totally innocent of any trafficking.

When he got to the part about the hack saw blade, neither he nor I could come up with the word for saw blade. Finally, he made a sawing motion with his hand and said, "inaww-inaww". We got the message. Even the district attorney laughed out loud and I thought his secretary, Esther, would wet her pants.

The laughter died quickly when the district attorney told him, "You will be escorted to the Big Jail. Mrs. McGill will give you a list of attorneys. Thank you very much. That will be all." We were dismissed.

Two policemen walked in and one slapped the handcuffs on Michael. He turned to me and casually offered, "Tell'em I'll give them the pick-up truck if they'll let me go."

"They already have your pick-up truck, Michael," I answered.

Rose and I walked to the patrol car with him and the two policemen. I suggested to him, "Let me call your father. Maybe he can help you out of this situation."

"No, no, no!" He almost panicked. "My Dad has a serious heart condition and this would just about do him in," but he said to Rose, "Call Hans in Amsterdam."

I never had the opportunity to see Michael again. Rose came to the office the next day to tell me he had been transferred to Puente Grande in Guadalajara. She said she hadn't been able to reach Hans.

All this happened at the time Consul Paul Kline was Chief of American Services at the Consulate General in Guadalajara. I've known some cranky, snotty-nosed, son-of-a-bitching consuls in my time, but Paul was a gem. I used to call him up and ask, "How're you doing today, Paul?" He would always answer, "I'm so busy I don't know which way my pecker's pointing! What do you need?"

I think Paul was a frustrated FBI agent. He loved to watch America's Most Wanted on television. One day he told me, "You know, I don't think the prisoner Michael is who he says he is."

"Why do you think that? What reason do you have?" I asked.

"Pure hunch. There's something about him and his wife that is plucking at me."

Paul invited the Regional Security Officer to make a prison visit with him. They went on a conjugal visiting day hoping to run into Rose. They got lucky.

When they saw Rose and Michael together, they knew they had their man. Later Paul sent me a video tape of America's Most Wanted show where Michael was the featured character.

Michael had made friends with a man named Jim. He was jealous of the fact that Jim had more money than he did and decided to rob him. He invited him to his house for a game of tennis and ended up murdering him.

Michael stabbed Jim twenty-six times with a kitchen knife and then he called in two buddies to get rid of the body while he cleaned up the mess.

It was never made clear where Rose was during this bloody game.

They took Jim's body in a pick-up truck to an abandoned military site. They devised handmade explosives, which they attached to the body and the truck. Their plan was to blow all evidence into smithereens, which could never be identified. They almost succeeded, but Jim's torso was blown aside.

The trail finally led back to Michael. He was found guilty and sentenced, strangely enough, to twenty-six years imprisonment. After attempted escapes from various California prisons, he was labeled as a high risk prisoner and admitted to Folsom State Prison, one of our countries' top security penitentiaries.

Somehow Michael's records were tampered with and he was failed to be listed as a high risk. He was allowed visitors and he was assigned to an outside maintenance crew.

Rose was a great help to him. She contacted an old friend who agreed to help him make the break. She carried detailed instructions to Michael when she visited him.

Their friend's plan was to break into Folsom and then escape. All Michael had to do was follow him. Too simple? It was. Impossible? Quite the contrary. That's exactly what happened.

Michael escaped through a storm sewer drain, which opened into the American River. He swam the river to the other side where a rubber raft had been left for him. Five months later he showed up in Puerto Vallarta.

Mexico and some other countries started the Prisoner Exchange Program in the early eighties. If you were being held in a foreign prison, and were facing an extended lock-up time, you could be eligible for a transfer back to your home country to serve out your sentence.

Michael didn't even know about this program, but one day the consular officer told him he was being processed for an exchange.

He knew how much trouble it had been to escape the California jails and he didn't want to go back home, so he killed one of his Mexican prison-mates. According to Mexican law, that canceled his chance for a transfer. Now he was a big time criminal in the United States *and* Mexico.

I don't know how he did it and the Mexican government never publicly shared this information, but he escaped Puente Grande. He is still on America's Most Wanted list, and it's believed he may still be in Mexico or another Latin country.

I got caught on another translating job, which was the biggest embarrassment of my life. Guadalupe Pulido was now the presiding judge where Judge/Chief of Police Salazar had sat. He called me to his office one day and asked me to translate for the owner of *The Shadow*.

This boat owner was being accused of raping a young Irish girl on the high seas. She had hired on as a mate on his sailboat, *The Shadow.* I'll never know why girls do this, but she did. I think there is supposed to be some code of honor between fishermen, boatmen and liars. The code of honor was broken in this case.

There are no jury trials in Mexico. District attorneys or judges make a decision, and that's it. There is a procedure where the offended files a formal complaint with the district attorney against the offender. This is called a *Demanda.* The district attorney sends out his policemen to arrest the defendant. Both the claimant and the defendant have a chance to tell their stories, but there comes a day when they have to come face-to-face. This is called *El Careo.* The day of *El Careo* had come and I was the translator.

The defendant and the claimant spoke English, but not Spanish. Judge Pulido didn't speak English. The *Careo* went like this:

Judge: "Mr. Shadow, you are accused of raping this young woman. What do you have to say?"

Shadow: "Nasuh, I didn't rape huh."

Judge: "Miss Irish Girl, what do you have to say?"

Irish Girl: "He did, Mr. Judge. He invited me to hire on as mate on his boat. We were going to sail to Acapulco. There was not much wind when we left, so we used the motor for a while. The motor conked out and we were afloat for a long time. We were floating toward the Tres Marias Islands and I knew that was prohibited because there's a federal prison out there. I was afraid and that's when it happened. We were just floating out there and he raped me."

Judge: "Mr. Shadow, you have heard the accusation. What do you have to say?"

Shadow: "Nasuh, Mr. Judge. I never raped huh. I just stuck my finger in. She was wearing a Tampax."

Judge: "What'd he say? What'd he say?"

Judge Pulido was looking straight at me and I was looking straight at a snow covered mountain framed print hanging on the wall above his head; wishing I were on that mountain. I could hear the court reporters snickering in their corner. Everybody else was silent, all eyes on me.

Me: "He said he didn't rape her, Mr. Judge. He said she was wearing a Tampax."

Judge: "Tampax? Tampax? What do you mean by Tampax?"

After I haltingly explained what a Tampax was and why and when it was used, all the time staring at that snow covered mountain print, he said, "She still accuses him of rape."

I closed my eyes, shook my head and said, "Mr. Judge, he says he only stuck his finger in."

The next day the head lines blazed in two-inch bold black print:

JENNY MCGILL DICE: "SOLAMENTE SE METIO SU DEDO!"

CHAPTER ELEVEN

Dames On My Path

I can think of many women whom I admire and highly respect; women in my own family, and those of my husband's. The list is long and will never be complete, but here is a starter: (Read as if they were written in the plural.)

Ana, Angelina, Barbara and Betty, Clyde, Catherine, Dolores, Francis and Fatima, Genia, Hilda, Irene, Juana, Joy, Jacqueline and Judy, Kay, Lynn and Lucy, Maria, Mercedes, Missy, Margo, Natalie, Ofelia, Paulina, Polly, Quimire, Ruth and Rachel, Sandra and Suzanne, Theresa, Violeta, Xaviera, Yolanda and Zelda.

A group of us English speakers used to get together frequently over a cup of mountain-grown coffee or a shot of home-brewed spirits made from a wild plant that looks a bit like the *agave* cactus, but it is called *lechuguilla*. We called ourselves The Hill-Top Intellectual Club. I don't know that we spoke very intelligently, but we could pass an entire afternoon discussing John Guare's popular stage play, *Six Degrees of Separation*. Guare's theory is that if you have met, or even seen John F. Kennedy, then everybody you know is separated by one degree from JFK. If this theory holds true, all of you are separated by two degrees from Eleanor Roosevelt, Queen Elizabeth and *Señora* Miguel Aleman, the wife of a former President of Mexico. I actually served tea to *Señora* Aleman and Eleanor. *Señora* Aleman was much prettier, and more gracious than Eleanor, but Queen Elizabeth was the most charming of all.

In 1983 we received word the Queen of England was coming to town. Puerto Vallarta was in shambles that year. The road to the airport was so full of pot-holes that Jesus Scherman, tour guide, explained to a complaining tourist, "Normally, this road is perfectly smooth, but we were hit with a meteorite shower last week." Sure, we were, Jesus. Happens every day in some of these towns.

Aurelio Rodriguez Garza was the city mayor, and he began ordering the people in Puerto Vallarta, "Paint the front of your houses! Fill in the pot-holes! Clean up the streets!" Those of you who may know him won't believe this, but I actually saw him pick up a broom, and sweep a portion of the main downtown plaza to kick off a major clean-up campaign.

Admiral Ortega was officially in charge of security and protocol, from the moment the Queen left Acapulco, where she first arrived, until she sailed from Puerto Vallarta.

He delighted us with his account of how she would leave Acapulco on her Royal Barge at the Royal Hour of ten o'clock in the morning, escorted by a brigade from the Mexican Navy. That brigade was named the Royal Escort. They would navigate through Royal Waters, named so because she was passing through them. They would arrive at, what had been designated as, the Royal Beach for a Royal Picnic. It was at this point that his fascinating wife, Yoya interjected,

"Yes, my dear, is that the way it will be? What'll you do if a Royal Mosquito comes out of jungle and bites her on her Royal Arse?"

Queen Elizabeth had requested to meet some English school children. We had none in Puerto Vallarta, but there was a British School in Mexico City, so a bus load of school kids were imported from there. Great Britain sponsors an orphanage in Zamora, Michoacan, so forty Mexican kids from the orphanage were also bussed in.

Arturo Musi was Director of Tourism at that time. I think the only English person living in Puerto Vallarta then was his wife, and she was still in hospital recuperating from the birth of their first child. Arturo called and asked me to help.

First of all, we need a place to house the eighty kids and their chaperones for a few hours before their audience with the Queen, and we also needed to feed and water them. Las Gaviotas was a swank, new residential neighborhood, which boasted a club house, kitchen facilities, and a swimming pool. It seemed like the perfect place to coral these little visitors for a few hours, and the club house manager was happy to cooperate in anything that would make the Queen happy.

What to do about food? I knew only two Canadians, and I thought they might like to get in on the act. After all, weren't the Canadians only one or two degrees away from the Queen?

I called Shirley Romero and Beverly Brauhn. They agreed to provide sandwiches, sodas and cookies for about ninety hungry mouths. Shirley had some idea of what we were up against, since she had worked in the tourist bureau at one time. Beverly just went along for the ride and a free lunch.

Shirley rounded up their Canadian friends to smear mayonnaise on bread. She convinced dear Tina Gutierrez Rizo to donate bread, ham, cheese and cookies for the kids. They coerced their friends into buying the sodas and we were set.

Musi had invited me to the Royal Welcoming Ceremony in the city hall. Now came the time to decide what to wear. I had stored away, as a souvenir of fancier times, a pair of elbow length, white leather gloves. The only hat I owned was made of straw, which I wore on the beach every so often. The cut-off Levis, the shorts, and the spaghetti-strap dresses, which made up my main wardrobe, seemed inappropriate. I flew to Houston in search of a dress that wouldn't embarrass the U.S. Government. I found one in Jacque Penne, a store that used to be called J.C. Penny, but their price tags had elevated the name. I bought a pair of short, white cotton gloves, but I couldn't find what I thought would be a suitable hat, so I flew back home with my new dress and gloves.

All of us worked hard to present the Queen with what she had requested. We pampered those kids. They ate, swam, played games, took their showers and put their uniforms back on. They were ready to be off to see the Queen. The English School kids dressed in white blouses, green and white plaid pants or skirts, and wore heavy green sweaters. The Zamora orphanage kids were more sensible. They wore simple white skirts or pants and white tops, and no sweaters.

I wore my Jacque Penne dress and carried my gloves in hand just in case the occasion arose to put them on. I had no hat. John Huston had sent me a floral arrangement the day before, after playing poker at our house. At the very last moment, I plucked a purple flower from the arrangement, pinned it in my hair and set off to rub sleeves with royalty.

We were seated in a special conference room upstairs in City Hall. Hot television camera lamps and over-head spots melted our make-up, turned the hair gel we had applied into a gummy mess, and caused our clothes to look as if they had been slept in. The English ladies didn't look much better either. They wore short, white cotton gloves, and I feel sure they bought their hats on the beach in Acapulco.

I was tired from my morning with the kids. The heat was unbearable, but I was impressed.

Admiral Ortega was decked out in full-dress white uniform, complete with sword and scabbard at his side. He also wore white gloves which were a little bit longer than ours. I don't remember if Aurelio wore a suit and tie or not. Surely, he must have. I do remember those over-head lights shining down on his sweating, bald head.

The Queen wore white gloves and one of her custom-made queenly hats. The biggest brooch I have ever seen was pinned to the lapel of the pale green suit she wore. The lamps caught its brilliance, and turned the room into a kaleidoscope of flashing emeralds, rubies, and diamonds.

Prince Philip was there, but he didn't sit by the Queen. Those places of honor were reserved for Admiral Ortega and Aurelio.

After the Queen was given a key to the city, and all the speeches were made, there was to be a walk around the plaza. I had managed to get out of the crowd as everybody was leaving the Royal Audience Room, and Musi and I were waiting downstairs in City Hall when the Queen and her entourage descended the stairs. As they started for the door to leave City Hall and make their Royal Plaza Walk, Musi said to me, "Come on, Jenny, let's walk with them."

"No, no, Musi, we can't do that!"

He said, "Sure we can. Come on! We may never get this opportunity again in our lives!" So we queued up directly behind Prince Philip and one of the ladies-in-waiting and joined Her Nibs in the Royal Plaza Walk.

Puerto Vallarta owns a fancy tour bus, which I've only seen on two occasions. Once was when President Richard Nixon came to visit, and the other, when Queen Elizabeth came to town. After our Royal Walk around the Royal Plaza, she and her official gang boarded the bus and were driven down Main Street. Oh, yes. The famous white glove was waving to the hoards of people lined up along the street to get a glimpse of Real Royalty. Musi and I didn't get on the bus.

That was one super-gracious lady. She put Eleanor Roosevelt to shame.

I love the Navy. If I had my life to re-do, I might even join the Navy. Women have been in the Navy many years. During World War II, they were called Waves. We had Bams in the Marines, Wacs in the Army, and Waves in the Navy. These women joined our military forces to serve their country during a world-wide crisis. Many of them served as secretaries or nurses on foreign soil, but none of them were ever in combat. That has changed also.

One day a U.S. Coast Guard ship came to visit Puerto Vallarta. Protocol dictated that the Mexican Navy send out a liaison officer to meet and greet the captain of all visiting ships. One of my job requirements was to go along on this Meet and Greet Mission. Normally, the visiting ship would come to dock, put the gang plank down and we could easily board.

This particular time, there was no space at the dock. Lieutenant Mario and I went out in one of the Navy launches, with a boatman at the wheel, to meet the ship. I had previously boarded a U.S. Navy ship at sea, so this was nothing new to me. That ship had put down a metal stairway which was fixed stably to one side of the ship. The worst part was getting off our launch onto the first step of the stairway, as the waves tossed us up and down alongside the ship. I had managed that, so I thought I could do it again if need be.

This time was different. The Coast Guard crew threw a rope ladder over the side for us to climb on board. I always dressed appropriately for these adventures, in pants and tennis shoes. Lieutenant Mario was watching the maneuvers through binoculars as we approached. He told me, "They've let down the rope ladder. That is the way we'll have to board."

I leaned over to one side of the launch and told him, "No way, Lieutenant! I'm not about to climb up a rope ladder to get aboard that ship! You go alone! Or radio that captain he can come down here to see me! I'm not climbing up a rope ladder!"

He continued scanning the horizon with his binoculars. "You have to go, Jenny. There are women on board."

He sent me up the rope ahead of him, and he was one rung behind me all the way. Thank God, there was no high wind to sway that rope ladder anymore than the rocking waves did. It was not as bad going up as coming down. Going up, I could focus on the side of the ship and the sky above me. Coming down, I had to look where I was putting my foot, and there was nothing except deep water to catch me if I made a misstep on the ladder. Lieutenant Mario went down first. I don't know if he thought he was protecting me or not, but if I had missed a rung, I would have knocked both of us into the water. Coast Guard ships are famous for their rescue missions.

Another time, a US Navy ship came to visit. These ships were usually coming off a long sojourn at sea, headed back to home port in San Diego, and they would pull in to Puerto Vallarta for a few days of R&R, Rest and Recreation, before going on. Many times, if dock space was available, the captain would host a cocktail party or luncheon on board for local Navy and city officials. Sometimes, they would hold Open House so the townspeople could come aboard. Children especially enjoy this treat.

The USS Duncan arrived, and she was captained by a woman. Gone were the secretary and nurse days of the Waves, Bams, and Wacs. Women are big stuff in our Navy these days. We even have women who carry the rank of Admiral.

This was not the first time the USS Duncan had visited. Ted Tedeshchi was the captain on the first visit. Captain Ted would be remembered by many in Puerto Vallarta, if for no other reason than his calling card. It showed a caricature drawing of a Navy captain pulling a big ship by a rope, as if it were his little red wagon. The captain had a long nose and huge feet. People who received his card loved it, and called him Captain Big Foot. He wore a size 15 shoe.

A very smart looking, white uniformed Captain Anne White welcomed us aboard. Being welcomed aboard a U.S. Navy ship is truly heady stuff. You walk to the edge of the ramp, a boatswain blows his whistle, calls out your name and title, and you walk proudly up the ramp. All officers are at attention and saluting you. I don't think civilians are supposed to salute back, but nobody ever told me not to do so, therefore I did.

As we arrived on deck, we met face-to-face with a bigger than life size cut-out photo of Captain Ted. He was now the Admiral of the Third Fleet, based in Hawaii. Those of us who had met him on the Duncan's previous visits were delighted, and we all cried out, almost as a chorus, "There's Captain Big Foot!"

Captain White had brought Operation Handclasp on her ship, and after a tour of the ship; she, the Mexican liaison officer, and I met in her quarters to organize off-loading and delivery of Operation Handclasp items.

It is difficult to say whether Operation Handclasp originated in Pusan, South Korea or Enid, Oklahoma, USA.

In July of 1950 Thomas E. Wood was called back into active military duty. Wood had been a cryptographer in World War II. He had obtained the rank of Colonel. He had been awarded the Bronze Star, Purple Heart and Commendation Medal. He was now serving as chaplain to the 325th Hospital Training Reserve Unit.

He was trained at Letterman Army Hospital in San Francisco and was commissioned as 2nd Lieutenant in the Medical Service Corps. In September, 1951 he was sent to South Korea as company commander of an ambulance company.

A few days after his arrival, one of the company ambulances struck a child, severely injuring him. The following day, Wood went to the make-shift hospital to see the child, and was utterly appalled by what he saw. Kids were lying, two to a litter, foot to foot on a dirty floor. Some of them were clothed only in a ragged piece of cloth used as a blanket. The doctors and nurses were overworked and lacked even the basic medical supplies.

Wood returned to his quarters after this sickening sight, and fired off a letter to his Alma Mater, Phillips University in Enid, Oklahoma. He wrote directly to the Dean of the Graduate Seminary and pleaded for help. He described the sorry conditions he had found in Pusan, and suggested that the student ministers appeal to their churches in Oklahoma and Kansas for donations of diapers, clothing, and blankets, medical and cleaning supplies. Anything would help.

Myron Neal, president of the Seminary Student Council worked a miracle and called it Operation Handclasp. The Phillips students organized a week-long drive to collect clothing and money for needy Korean children. They were successful. Five tons of clothing and $1500 dollars were collected.

In mid-October of that year, Wood's commander received a call from the Army Post Office at the Pusan port, asking that Lieutenant Tom Wood be sent down with a 2 ½ ton truck to pick up the mail. That was the first of many truck loads of over-the-counter medicines, toys, diapers, basic medical supplies, canned staples and such to be shipped to all parts of the world.

Operation Handclasp is not a military operation. It is, as its name implies, a gesture of good will. Military and Coast Guard vessels are used to transport the donations.

Fifty-four years later, Operation Handclasp is bigger than ever. It has its own headquarters in San Diego, and the last I heard, it was directed by a Navy Captain, but it's not Navy, not Air Force, not Army, nor Coast Guard. It is Operation Handclasp.

I have met some wonderful women on my path, but there was one woman I would have preferred to take another road.

She publicly disapproved, via newspapers, of a segment of the American community who had accepted an invitation to attend a forum presided over by her husband's political opponent.

She claimed we were foreigners meddling in her adopted country's affairs. That was not the case. She wasn't Mexican either. We would have gone to her husband's forum if he had thought of inviting us, but he didn't. As an afterthought, when he did invite us, we dutifully and respectfully attended. She also made it very clear in her letter that she wouldn't have any "dealings" with me in the future.

Many of my friends, both Mexican and American, expressed their desire to answer her letter in kind, but I dissuaded them from doing so. They were quick to understand that we would be dignifying her letter if we answered publicly.

At that time I was not aware that she wouldn't follow diplomatic protocol, nor consult with her predecessors regarding visiting foreign naval vessels.

"Take your flowers and bottle of wine and shove it!" That's what she and her husband did the day the US Navy ship brought in Operation Handclasp. They told us the people in their flooded homes from the previous day's storm didn't need dry food, blankets or medicine. They told us the people didn't need our help in digging out from those mud slides we had that day. If I remember correctly, her husband was quoted as saying, "Where do you think we are, Biafra?"

Ever the reigning diplomat in situations such as this, the Admiral of the 12th Naval Zone smoothed their feathers, and told them they would accept the Operation Handclasp goods. He informed them that his men would deliver the items to the neediest neighborhoods. He also advised them he would need a signed receipt for all goods delivered.

The three years she and her husband ruled Puerto Vallarta were not pleasant ones. Perhaps they both have fallen off the road somewhere. She didn't make my list of Most Admired Women.

CHAPTER TWELVE

Darling Little Ones

My friend, Georgia Stasi says, "I love babies. But then they grow up and sometimes they are not so sweet anymore."

When we first moved to Puerto Vallarta, there were no American babies. We were the geriatric jet setters. Nobody who was young enough to be producing babies had enough money to be here. We were retirees or dropees. Dropees might have had an interest in the process of reproduction, but The Pill had already been developed and no educated, moralistic, fine upstanding lady ever made plans to vacation in Mexico without starting on The Pill. Nowadays, they also include a condom in their handbags. Even some young Mexican schoolgirls include them in their book satchels. Not enough of them do to cut down on the madre soltera statistics, but some do. We have plenty of single mothers in the United States and Canada, but Mexico wins, hands down.

When job opportunities began to open for the foreigners, Registration of an American Citizen Born Abroad forms were supplied. Phil Ober only registered one baby in all those years he worked as consular agent, but it was a booming business with me.

State Department policies change, as everything else does. An American mother, who had lived in the states for five years after the age of twelve, could automatically transfer American citizenship to her child. That child could be born anyplace in the world and it didn't matter if the mother was married to the father or not. This was not true for the American father. He had to be legally married to the child's mother, or to be able to present pretty strong proof that he truly was the father of the child.

John Johnson, sit back and enjoy a good read. You are famous. As much as I dislike you, I have to include you in this book.

Many foreigners live in Yelapa, but you never see much of them, unless you spend the night in the thatched roof hotel on the beach. They stay in their own thatched roof houses until the tourist boat leaves in the afternoon to return to Puerto Vallarta. Then they come out of the wood-work like termites.

John and his lover lived in Yelapa for several years. His friend died from cirrhosis of the liver, but John continued to live there. One day he and a Mexican woman came to the office with a baby girl. John declared that he was the natural father of this baby and wanted to register her as an American citizen. I explained to him what the policy was and the reason why I couldn't register the child since he was not even married to the mother. Angrily, he said, "I can fix that!" and he stomped out the door.

Within an hour, he and the woman were back with the baby. He shoved a marriage certificate over the counter and growled at me, "Now do it! You don't have an excuse!"

I was in no mood to deal with his anger or stubbornness that day, so I told him, "Sorry, John, I don't feel competent to handle this case. You'll need to go to Guadalajara to register this birth." This angered him even more.

He did go to the Consulate General. He accused me of refusing to register his baby at the Consular Agency in Puerto Vallarta. Naturally, the consul wanted to know why, so he called me. I told him why I doubted that John was the father. We knew that it was probably biologically possible, but not very likely. The consul suggested we investigate this case a bit. He thought it would be wise to go to Yelapa and visit with some of the Mexican neighbors to try to determine if they knew anything about a close relationship between John and his Mexican woman.

I sent Jackie. Being Mexican, I figured she could nose around Yelapa without attracting too much attention. Jackie was to contact Our Man in Yelapa first to see if he knew anything about these people. Over the years, she had made friends with other people in the village and she had a much better chance of finding out something than I did. She pretended she was a tourist for the day, hung a camera around her neck and took the tourist boat to Yelapa.

Jackie was a good detective. She walked into the office the next morning with a smug look on her face, "I don't think so, *Señora* Jenny."

From what the natives told Jackie, John had taken in another lover after his first one died. The woman, who gave birth to the child that John was claiming to be his, actually was his cleaning lady. The people with whom Jackie had spoken told her that this woman had several other children, but no husband.

The consuls in Guadalajara made the final decision based on what Jackie reported after her visit to Yelapa. The baby was denied American citizenship.

After a few good insults, John walked out of the Consulate in a rage. He flew to San Diego and filed a law suit against the Department of State, Consulate General and me. I had never had a law suit against me before, so I thought it rather exciting. I've known other people who have sued the Department of State and won. John didn't.

Many years passed. I had retired from the Consular Agency. Howard, friends Walter Bauman, Mario Alberto and I were in a park one Sunday morning in Guadalajara. Walter spoke to a man he knew and the man asked him, "Are you still running around with this trash?" as he nodded toward me.

The four of us stood there, stunned. The man turned and walked away. He returned shortly, holding a girl approximately twelve years old, by the arm. She was trying to pull away from him, crying, "Don't, Daddy, don't, you're hurting me. Let me go!" He screamed at her, "I want you to take a good look at this bitch! She's the woman who kept you from being an American citizen! Just look at her!" I had not recognized John.

Ann and Ed Aster by-passed me and went directly to Guadalajara to register their baby. Ann was nearing menopause age. She and Ed were of Norwegian descent and had very light complexions. The baby boy's skin was just dark enough to cause the consul doubt.

He sent Ann to an obstetrician to ascertain if she had given birth recently. Yes, she had, but, the doctor couldn't determine how recently.

Once again, the consul asked me to do some detective work. At this time, Judy Galeana was volunteering much of her time at the Consular Agency, so off we went like Brenda Starr with her side-kick.

We drove to the neighborhood where the Asters lived and chatted with neighbors and shopkeepers. Some of the folks said that they had seen Ann while she was pregnant. Others said they had never noticed her being pregnant.

We went to the small clinic where the baby, supposedly, had been born. We asked to see the patient records for March 19, 1984, the day the baby was reported to have been born. There were two patients listed in the maternity ward on that date and Ann was one of them. There was a notation that the two patients and one baby had left the hospital that day.

Birthing a baby in a Mexican hospital and leaving the same day is not uncommon. I visited the Doctora, who had, supposedly, attended Ann's delivery. I asked her to show me her patient record to see how many visits Ann had made before March 19, 1984. There was an entry that she visited the Doctora two times, including the day she registered at the clinic. That is not too uncommon with Mexican women either. However, most American women of Ann Aster's age would have a long record of pre-natal care. She didn't.

The information that we gathered was sent on to the Consulate General. The consuls decided this was a valid registration and issued the baby a U.S. Passport.

Sometimes people die all alone in this country. No family, no friends, nobody. In those cases, I always tried to get somebody to come along with me to accompany the body to the cemetery. Once again, Bob and Elena Gollum and I stood around while the grave-digger was filling in the grave. His wife and I started up a conversation. She said to me, "We have a little American baby buried here."

How could that be? All American deaths were reported to me and I had never worked a baby's death. The woman led me over to a grave with a tiny tombstone on it. It read: Baby Aster, born March 19, 1984, died March 19, 1984.

Of course, I was instructed to go back to Ann and Ed Aster's and pick up the baby's passport to cancel it. I didn't want to face them, so I sent Poor Judy and Howard to do the dirty work. Poor Judy was as much a cry-baby as I was. With tears streaming down her face, she reported that when she told Ann why they were there, Ann called back inside to her husband, "Oh, Eddie, they're saying Tony is not ours."

That mother doesn't like me either. But she still has her Mexican baby also.

This incident became the talk of the Foreign Service Corp and was used in the training courses to point out how careful one needed to be in registering babies.

Luz and Tony Tuck carefully avoided any of these problems. They were not married, but had been living together for several months. They were our personal friends. Another Thanksgiving Day had rolled around and I invited them to dinner.

They were all smiles when they arrived and joyfully told us they were expecting a baby. We toasted the new parents-to-be while another guest snapped the camera.

Throughout Luz' pregnancy Tony would take her picture. She posed for him with her tummy poked out to its' full-blown beauty. She even posed for him in the delivery room, wearing her obstetric leggings. There was no question about her birthing a baby, but she was Mexican.

Since I knew for sure they had been living together prior to the birth, my supervisor asked me to write an affidavit attesting to what I knew, which I did. We sent Luz's pictures along with the affidavit and Birth Report form.

Young Travis would be issued a U.S. Passport later. I had developed the custom of giving a small American flag to all the American children who had been born that year at our 4th of July celebration. He and his mom were still in the hospital and couldn't come to the party. I gave the flag to a very proud Texas grandmother.

It came to my attention recently that Mr. and Mrs. Stanley Black, and their family had donated a Healing and Meditation Garden to Children's Hospital in Los Angeles.

About twenty-five years ago, Stanley Black and his fishing buddies played a big role in the healing of a group of kids from El Tuito, another village down the road south of Puerto Vallarta.

Mr. Black, friends and associates started what they called The Stanley Black Fishing Tournament. They came to Puerto Vallarta, sans spouses, and stayed at the Camino Real Hotel before it became a Dream Hotel. I don't know how much fishing they did, but they played a bit of poker.

At the time, Toody Walton was the editor of *Vallarta Today*, an English version of *Vallarta Opina*. She had run a story of an accident involving the children. Black's group read the story and decided they would donate their week's poker winnings to the needs of the children.

It seems that Mr. Black was not only generous, but very street smart. He didn't want the money to go to the fathers' desires, but toward the kids needs. A special fund was set up and administered by the town's treasurer. The mother of each child could withdraw money as needed, but the father couldn't touch it.

We learned that at least three of the kids needed to be transferred to a hospital in Guadalajara.

Brian Johnson had flown his plane in from Mexico City to visit with Ken and Pat Flanery. Brian flew evacuee choppers for our downed pilots in Viet Nam and Cambodia for Air America during the Viet Nam War, often under heavy fire. He offered to take the seats out of his plane and fly another mercy mission from Puerto Vallarta.

Pat and I made arrangements for this transfer with the director, doctors, nurses and social workers at Regional Hospital. While Brian was filing a flight plan, Pat and I went to the hospital to meet with Dr. Eleazar Carrazco.

There they lay. Three little brown charred bodies spread-eagled on their cots. Their burned clothes had been stripped from them and their mothers hovered anxiously by their side. Intravenous solutions were dripping into their tiny arms. They were sedated, but their eyes were wide-open and watching every movement in their room.

They had been in Tomas' home in El Tuito preparing for little Laura's birthday party. Mama had been making a hot fruit punch for the adults. Unfortunately, she walked out of the room. Little kids like to help in the kitchen. Pepito climbed up onto a chair to check out the punch's progress, which was setting on top of an open alcohol burner. He thought it might need a bit more *aguardiente* and recalling the rest of story still hurts.

Dr. Carrazco and his paramedics readied the kids for the trip to the airport in the ambulance. Pat and I followed along behind the ambulance and on to the tarmac at the private terminal where Brian's plane was waiting. As gently as possible, each child and his attached bottle of intravenous solution was lifted off his gurney and placed in the plane. Dr. Carrazco planned to accompany them to the Guadalajara hospital.

At the last minute, Pat threw me the car keys and yelled out, "Call Ken, tell him I'll be home later! I'm going with 'em!" She climbed into the plane alongside the kids.

She told me later she asked little Laurita what she wanted for her birthday when she got out of the hospital.

"A yellow dress" was her answer.

I'm sure Pat has bought as many yellow dresses for little girls as I have since that day, but the scars are still there.

But they lived. They're scarred too, but they lived, thanks to Stanley Black, his friends and Brian Johnson.

The worst baby story I ever heard: Carl and Jolene had been married several years and had no children. Doctors told Jolene she probably never would have kids. They came to Puerto Vallarta on vacation with the idea of inquiring about adopting a baby. They made friends with other American residents and in their conversations expressed their desire to adopt. Their new friends advised them, "Don't do that! There is so much paperwork involved in adoption. We can help you buy a baby." And they helped.

The story unraveled over the next few months. A Mexican woman fell in love with one of our local policemen. They became roommates. A few days after they set up housekeeping, she began to be extremely nauseated in the early mornings. Not too unusual, but a wee bit strange, especially so early in the game. Mr. Cop told her, "I think you're knocked-up, and I don't think I did it. Keep my clothes clean and have food on the table when I come in. When your baby comes, give it away."

Remember we are living in a religious environment where abortion is generally out of the question. Even macho cops respect a pregnant woman most of the time. The expectant mother made arrangements with a woman friend to take the baby when it arrived. Time passed, the birth was normal and mother officially registered the child at Civil Registry in the city hall. Then she gave her baby to her friend.

Her friend wanted to have no problems in the future about whose child this was. She also went to Civil Registry office and registered the baby as her own. She later became involved in an illegal money scam called the Pyramid Game, similar to the old Ponzi Game. Before she went to jail, she gave the baby to another friend.

That friend didn't know how long she would be able to keep the baby in her care, but she wanted it to be properly registered. This was the third time the baby visited the Civil Registry office in City Hall. Each time she went, she got a new name and a new mother.

This newest mother ran a very lucrative business, locally called the Tacon Dorado trade, or the Golden Heel business. It is the oldest profession in the world and, by the way, it's legal in Mexico.

The baby was used by the girls to attract the men passing by the brothel. They would hold the baby upside down, by her feet, out the window, so the men could fondle and kiss the baby until they were aroused enough to be more than eager to go inside and spend their money on adult entertainment.

The story goes that an off-duty policeman happened to be wandering through that neighborhood one night and saw the baby dangling from the window. He investigated further and subsequently, the baby was taken into custody by DIF.

Lacking an orphanage where adoption procedures were available, Carl and Jolene were advised by their new friends to make an inquiry at DIF. It just so happened that the officials at DIF knew of a baby who needed a home and they were willing to help Jolene.

According to what Jolene told me, she paid $2,500 dollars to the director of DIF, not the president but the director, who was a doctor. The good doctor put the baby into her arms and said, "She is yours now."

Mama No 4, Jolene, knowing that she would need a birth certificate before applying for a U. S. Passport for her new baby, registered her at Civil Registry in the city hall as her natural born child. Then she made a trip to the Consulate General to apply for the passport for the child. The consuls immediately tripped her up in her story and told her, "Follow the rules or you'll never enter the United States with this baby."

That is when I met them: Carl, Jolene, and Dana, the baby's fourth new name. All of this had been going on for weeks before I ever knew about it, but the media already had an account of what was happening.

I read about this in the early edition of the newspaper and was aghast. That same morning Carl and Jolene brought Dana into the office. Poor little baby was so malnourished she looked like a sack of bones. She had what looked like cigarette burns all over her body. Her baby lips were so misshapen they were grotesque. Jolene had already had her checked by a pediatrician and she was chock-full of amoeba, the intestinal bacteria so often found in the tropics.

Jolene put the baby up on the counter in the front office, laid her head down beside her and sobbed, "Please help me! I've tried everywhere else and nobody will help." Since I had read the newspaper earlier that morning, I knew we were in for a really tough time.

The three came into my office where Jolene poured out her heart. She was a postal clerk in a small northeastern state and her husband was an insurance salesman. They didn't have much money, but they wanted a child desperately. I never asked her why they didn't try to adopt in the United States. I wish I had. She told me what she had learned from the different officials with whom they had been dealing and about how this baby had been treated. She recounted the negative response she had gotten at the Consulate General and the local immigration officials.

Carl couldn't stay any longer in Puerto Vallarta with Jolene. He had extended his leave of absence beyond his company's patience and had to return to his job. He left Jolene and the baby in a rented apartment. On Sunday nights he flew the "red eye" special into New York, worked all week and returned to Puerto Vallarta the following Saturday to fly out again the next day.

For five weeks, Jolene would bring her baby to me every morning, lay her head on the counter and cry. I fought with the local immigration officials, my own immigration officials and consuls in Guadalajara and got absolutely nowhere. Rules are rules and must be followed. Damn the bureaucraps! Jolene would rant, rave, wail and cry. The baby would cry and I would cry. My bed pillow at home rotted from salty tears.

Mexican immigration officials suggested we start from ground zero and that Jolene and Carl could adopt the baby. The U. S. Immigration Chief in Guadalajara had also advised them to do the same. That meant we needed to determine who the real mother was. Was she the woman in jail, the cop's live-in, or the Madame of Tacon Dorado? Civil Registry records showed that baby Dana had four mamas, including Jolene. From what we had read in the newspaper and what we had heard through grape-vine sources, we decided the true mother was the cop's girl-friend. We needed to see her, so my other consular assistant, Luis Guillermo Rodriguez, and I left Jackie in the office and with Rafael Ventura, the body-guard, we made a social call.

I have no idea where we went, but Rafael knew the cop and knew where they lived. We pulled up in front of a tumbling down building with newspapers and cardboard boxes taped into the windows where panes used to be. Broken beer bottles and smashed aluminum soda cans were scattered everywhere.

When we got out of the car, we realized we were not alone. Ramon Gonzales Lomeli, Director of Tourism, was there and I was grateful for his company. A reporter and cameraman from one of the yellow-rag journals somehow had learned of our plans, so they were also there. I pleaded with them, "Please, boys, don't take pictures of this."

We entered a compound like none you have ever seen. It was a village within a village. There were four outside walls, which enclosed an area where maybe fifteen families lived. Cement laundry basins and scrub boards were set up in the center of the dirt courtyard. A piece of broken mirror was wired to a tree that stood nearby. The men could have a comfortable outdoor shave while they chatted with the women doing the laundry. There were four port-a-toilets set off toward the backside of the compound. They had no doors, but their entryways were covered with brightly colored, flowered oilcloth.

Naked-bottom toddlers were playing in the dirt. Some were eating fruit or munching on a dry tortilla. Others were crying because they had none. I didn't see any red wagons, tricycles, rubber balls, jump ropes or jacks. They played with old spoons, inner tubes and broken toy pistols.

Ramon introduced himself to a man standing in the courtyard and told him who we were and who we wanted to see. The man pointed to a cubbyhole; one of many around these four walls. None of the others had doors either. More colored oilcloth provided what privacy these folks needed. There must have been a strong code of honor within this compound.

We stood outside the oilcloth and called out, "Señor Elvira, *Señora* Elvira!" A young attractive woman, maybe in her early twenties, opened the curtain and stepped outside. Ramon explained to her who we were and why we had come. Yes, she had given her baby to a friend, but she didn't know the rest of the story.

I told her, "*Señora*, there is an American couple here who want to adopt your baby and take it to the United States, give her love, a good home and an education. Would you agree to the adoption?" Without a moment's hesitation, she said nonchalantly, "Fine by me." It was that simple.

There were documents that needed to be signed and witnessed, and we needed a flat surface to write on. She pushed the oilcloth curtain wide open and we stepped into her one-room cubbyhole.

With no windows, the only light came from the open curtain. An un-made, tousled double bed was pushed up against one wall. There was a small wooden table and two wooden straight-backed chairs. She had set up her kitchen in a corner near the doorway with a two-burner portable cook top set on a table with a galvanized bucket filled with water underneath. There were two unwashed plates, two coffee mugs, two forks and two spoons stuck into one of the mugs setting on the table.

Ramon, Luis Guillermo and I were quite taken aback when we scanned the back wall of this unkempt hovel. It was entirely filled, from top to bottom, with the most incredible state-of-the-art home entertainment center we had ever seen.

Unbelievable, but during all this stressful, emotional time, Jolene got pregnant! The kicker was that Mexican immigration laws prohibit folks from adopting babies if they can procreate on their own and the media was breathing down our necks. None of us dared to make a wrong move. Civil Registry and DIF were chewed up and spit out by the press on a daily basis for already breaking so many rules.

My consular assistants could see what this was doing to me, so they took matters into their own hands. I didn't know about this until after it happened, but they decided that Jackie should pay a call on *Señora* Alicia in the Immigration office. Jackie was a mother and *Señora* Alicia was a mother. They both held pretty responsible positions in federal offices. I suppose Jackie thought, as a Mexican mother to another Mexican mother, maybe they could come up with a solution.

A few days passed and Jolene and Dana didn't appear. I commented to Jackie and Luis Guillermo, "Wonder what's happened?" Both shrugged their shoulders, but made no comments. A few more days went by and still no sign of Jolene and Dana. As emotionally draining as their visits had been, I worried about them and wondered aloud, "What could have happened to them?"

Jackie and Luis Guillermo went into closed conference and decided to let me in on their game. Jackie confessed that she had met with *Señora* Alicia and begged her to help. Alicia told Jackie, "There is nothing I can do. I can't change the rules. The best advice you can give Jolene is to get on a bus with that baby and go to the border. Get off and walk across at night. She probably won't get caught. Take her outside of the Consular Agency to tell her this, Jackie." And that is exactly what happened.

I still receive a Christmas card from Carl and Jolene each year. Dana and Melinda are brown and white sisters growing up very nicely together.

I had the opportunity to speak with one of their teachers, who was vacationing in Puerto Vallarta, when they were still in kindergarten. She told me they both seemed to be equally bright and intelligent, but perhaps Dana might be a bit more aggressive than Melinda.

CHAPTER THIRTEEN

Dirty Old Men

Dirty old men and dear old men are sometimes one and same.

Perry Graystone was a semi-invalid, the consequences of a stroke. His thought process seemed to be about normal, but he was practically immobile. He spent most of his time in a wheelchair. He could get out of the wheelchair and walk to the bathroom or bed, but he used crutches equipped with metal braces, which fit over his forearms to give him more stability.

Perry was a handsome man; he still had a fine head of red hair and the bluest of blue eyes, but he was frail.

When I met Perry he was living in Hotel Marsol on Los Muertos Beach. The hotel seemed like an ideal spot for him. There was a bar and dining room. It was right on the beach, and it had an elevator, but the room security was lousy.

Somebody either broke into the room, or was invited in. It doesn't matter, but that someone beat poor old Perry black and blue one night, and stole his check book. The hotel manager called me.

Perry wasn't one of the Destitutes. He had a small monthly income from a company in Oklahoma from which he had retired, plus his Social Security. He could afford a caretaker and an up-grade in his life style.

We took care of the stolen checkbook problem, but he decided he wanted to live someplace away from the beach crowd.

One of the original hospitals in Puerto Vallarta had recently been converted into a supervised retirement home. The old Sanatorio Medico now had a new name. It was called Los Tabachines, and the walls had been painted. There was a half-assed dining room. It served mostly sandwiches, but, there was an elevator, and some of the rooms had kitchenettes. Perry thought this could be his new home.

Steve Wilson was a wonderful friend. When he wasn't suing somebody in the courts, he was bored. He came to me and asked if he could help in any way. "Wow! Steve, you can help me with Perry."

Steve, Perry and I had a Budget and Finance Committee meeting one morning. Perry told us what he wanted. We looked at his income and set up a budget. So many pesos for rent, so much for food, cigarettes, booze, and other minor essentials. Then we figured in a reasonable fee for a caretaker. Financially speaking, Perry could live pretty well.

Steve helped him make the move to his new quarters. Luis Guillermo lived near Los Tabachines. He put the word out in the neighborhood that Perry needed a part-time caretaker; someone who could help him with his bath, keep his room and clothes clean, and cook his meals.

I interviewed the lady who applied for the job. She was a pleasant, middle-aged woman, stable and responsible. She was hesitant about the cooking, but I assured her that Perry wasn't accustomed to gourmet dining; he could eat beans, rice, tortillas and soup, just like the rest of us. She accepted. Alma went to work for him.

His life was dull. He had no friends to come visit. He had a small black and white television, and enjoyed spy novels, murder mysteries, and porno. We tried to keep him supplied with reading material.

Steve made sure that all Perry's bills were paid up to date. He'd go on Friday mornings and sit with Perry and Alma as they planned the week's meals, and made sure Alma had enough money to buy whatever Perry wanted.

On rare occasions, Alma would call for a taxi, and take him to the Malecon, the board walk along the ocean front. This was a hassle for both of them. It was no easy matter getting Perry and his wheelchair in or out of a car. But it did offer a little diversion in his monotonous life.

I tried to get by for a visit about once a week. Sometimes I would take them a piece of pie or cake that I'd baked that week. I could see that Alma was keeping the place tidy, and Perry's clothes were clean and nicely ironed. She even trimmed his hair and clipped his fingernails. He never complained and he truly seemed appreciative that he was being looked after.

On one of these visits, Alma followed me out into the hall as I was leaving. I figured it was about time to increase her wages, and I was sure Perry would agree. When we were out of his hearing range, she sadly shook her head, "*Señora*, I just can't do it."

"Can't do what, Alma?" I asked. I had been thinking that everything was running along so smoothly, and I was ready to offer her a raise.

"I just can't go to bed with him, *Señora.*"

"Oh, lordy! Nobody expected you to do that! Just keep him clean and fed. We'll take care of the rest."

I phoned Steve and told him what Alma had said. We decided we should both go visit Perry together.

After telling Perry why we were there, I said to him, "Perry, I don't blame you. I think we can come up with a solution to this. I know exactly how much money you have. If you want a woman, you can afford one. Steve will find one for you. You pay her for her services, but keep your hands off Alma." So it was written into Perry's budget that he would have a weekly visit from a *Social Worker.*

Harvey Brocklyn wasn't destitute either, but he was another DOM. He came from Michigan. He was a big husky fellow and what hair he had left was red. The only reason I knew his name was Harvey and that he was from Michigan is that I saw his passport.

He had been a merchant marine, and the world knew him as Red Brocklyn.

Somewhere along the way Red had married a Mexican lady and they had a baby girl. There was no close relationship between Red and his daughter, although they both acknowledged their kinship. Kari was a thalidomide baby, and she had what looked like seal flappers for arms.

Hotel Marlyn is located on Avenida Mexico, as you come into town, and before you come to the Malecon. One Sunday morning the manager of this hotel called me to say one of his permanent guests had not left his room for several days, and he was drinking heavily. He also said he had fallen and his face was pretty badly bruised.

I called our American doctor, John Mabry. Dr. John had graduated from med school in Guadalajara, met a Vallarta native, married, and was trying to settle in to a normal life, after a wild four years in the big city.

Dr. John always reminded me of a country doctor in Rural Town, USA. I expected to see him sitting in a buggy, pulled by one horse, clippety-clopping down a dusty road. He should be dressed in a thin cotton black suit, sleeves too short for him, a white shirt, a black string tie, and a wide brimmed black hat pulled down over his ears. This was my Dr. John.

The manager let us into Brocklyn's room, and what we saw was not a pretty sight. His face looked as if he had been in the boxing ring the night before. He was sitting up in bed, and amazingly, his hair was combed and he had shaved. He might've been forewarned of our visit, I don't know.

Red had one of those nasty, feisty, little dogs in the bed with him. I think it must have been a cross between a Chihuhua and a Terrier. It had bulging eyes, which looked about like Red's did, and it would not stop yapping.

Dr. John did most of the talking that morning. He had met Brocklyn before. He knew exactly what he was dealing with. He knelt down on the floor, and pulled a half-empty bottle of vodka from under the bed. He went into the bathroom, and pulled another partially filled bottle from the commode tank. Another one was in the shower, and he found another one in the dirty clothes basket. Red hadn't bothered trying to hide the half-filled glass sitting on his bedside table.

My country doctor told him, "Red, we've been through this before. If you keep on like this, you're going to kill yourself."

"I don't really care, Doc," was his answer.

I was totally disgusted. I had heard from active AA members that you can't help an alcoholic until he decides he wants help. I didn't think Red wanted help yet.

I always carried a brown leather folder with me, which served as my briefcase. I kept certain forms in it that might come in handy while out on the job. I jerked the American Citizen's Death Abroad form out of my folder and snapped at him, "Well, let's just fill this thing our right now. It'll save me a lot of time in the future."

He opened the drawer of his bedside table, took out his U.S. Passport, and as he handed it to me he said, "It's all right there. Everything you need to know."

This man really doesn't care if he lives or dies.

"Red, tell me about your next-of-kin."

"Don't have any." He replied. I didn't know about Kari.

I asked him, "Well then, what do you want me to do with your body?"

He motioned toward his window to the ocean outside, and said "You can take me out there in a boat, and just drop me over the side."

I felt we couldn't carry this conversation much further, so Dr. John and I left.

A few weeks passed and Travis Flippen came to see me.

He and Red were long-time drinking buddies, but now Flip thought Red might be in trouble. The manager of Hotel Marlyn had asked Red to move out. He had rented a room in the neighborhood where Flip and his family lived. The landlady told Flip that Red never left his room. He would send one of the neighborhood kids out for vodka, milk, and a sandwich. He shared the sandwich and milk with his bug-eyed barking dog.

Flip was naturally concerned for his buddy. He said he had gone by the house and could see through the window into Red's bedroom. He thought Red must have cut his hand because his arm was hanging off one side of the bed, and the dog was licking his bleeding fingers.

He figured he might be able to sober Red up enough to get him on a plane back to Michigan. I enthusiastically wished him good luck.

Flip and Red had shared the stories of their former lives while tippling tequila. Flip knew Red had been married to a Mexican and that they had a daughter. He had never met the Mexican lady or the daughter. The mother had died before Flip met Red. He also knew he had an ex-wife and a grown daughter in Michigan, and he knew how to find the daughter, Janice. Somehow they got Red into a rehab center in Grand Rapids.

One day Red appeared at the Consular Agency in Puerto Vallarta. I almost didn't recognize him. He was close to being handsome. He had been on the wagon for six months. He told me he had made a deal with the director of the rehab center that if he promised to stay sober, he could be released and return to Puerto Vallarta. Somehow they involved me. His pension and Social Security checks were being mailed to the rehab center. The director had told him she would mail them to him in care of the Consular Agency.

That's what happened for a few months. Red would come by once a month to pick up his checks. He always looked well and swore he wasn't drinking, "Only a beer now and then with old Flip".

I would occasionally report to Miss Agnes that it seemed Red had truly recovered. We finally came to the conclusion he was a big enough boy he could handle his own mail now.

He decided he would move to Chapala. Chapala is a small town on Lake Chapala which is the biggest lake in Mexico. It is loaded with English-speaking foreigners. I thought that would be the last I would see of him, and it was.

One day I received a call from Jose Luis Guillermo Palacios, at the Consulate General in Guadalajara. Palacios told me he had just come back to the office from visiting a man down in Chapala. He said the man was very sick and needed to be hospitalized, but was refusing to go. He told me that the man said, "I'll only go if Jenny McGill tells me to go." I asked Palacios who this man was. He said, "Red Brocklyn."

"You tell Red Brocklyn I said for him to get his butt in the hospital."

"Perdoname, *Señora*. You said what?"

I repeated, "Tell him I said to get his butt into the hospital! Now! Today!"

Red died within the week from pneumonia. He had given Kari and Janice as his next-of-kin.

The two daughters decided that since their dad had spent his working years on the water and chose to retire by the water, his remains should be cremated and disposed of at sea. This duty fell to Kari.

Kari collected the ashes from the mortuary in Guadalajara and brought them back to Puerto Vallarta. She decided to sit with them for a few weeks.

In the meantime, I received a letter from a Charlene Brocklyn. She claimed to be Red's first wife, from whom he was divorced. She wanted to tell me she knew about Kari through her daughter, Janice.

She wrote, "This is something Red never knew. Kari is his real daughter. Janice is not. I should know. I tell you this because there may be some way you can help Kari."

About a month or so passed and Kari came by to tell me she had taken a boat to Yelapa, and on the way she dropped Red's ashes over the side.

I asked her if Red was listed as her father on her Mexican birth certificate. "Oh, yes, Jenny. He and my mother registered me soon after I was born. They didn't think I was going to live, but they registered my birth."

"But did they ever register you as an American citizen?" I asked her.

"No, I don't think so. I don't have any papers that show they did."

"Did you ever find their marriage certificate in either of their files?"

"Their marriage certificate and my mom's death certificate were with Red's passport" she told me.

I don't know what I thought could happen, but I strongly believe in angels. "Kari," I said to her, "I think you ought to go back to Guadalajara. Take your birth certificate, your parents' marriage and death certificates, and take this sealed envelope with you. I don't know if you can get any help or not, but it is worth trying." I gave her the letter from Charlene Brocklyn.

Kari was subsequently registered as an American citizen, and she would be receiving a monthly check from Red's Social Security.

She now owns and operates a small day-care center for toddlers of working mothers.

The Dirtiest Old Man I ever met was called Dirty Cal. He was living here before we moved down. We would see him on the beach regularly. I never knew he had a last name. Sometimes he would be referred to as Old Cal, but generally it was Dirty Cal.

Dirty Cal had built his dream house high on a hillside, overlooking the entire Bay of Flags. His house no longer exists. It got in the way of road building equipment when the tunnel was built to carry the traffic around the town, not through it.

He had a girl friend called Jungle Jean. Her toe nails were about as long as her dirty finger nails. She had long, tousled, dish-water blond hair, going grey. She wore bikini bathing suits during the daytime and see-through gauzy dresses at night, which revealed every unattractive feature the woman ever had. She might have been rounded out in the right places at one time, but many hours of body-baking in the sun and age had taken their revenge on her.

Nevertheless, Jungle Jean was as much a party rat as Dirty Old Cal. They would spend their days on Los Muertos Beach. They invited everybody they met to 'come by for cocktails at seven tonight'.

I was only in that house one time on a social basis.

My friend, Sky Spalding, an artist from Colorado, was a winter-time resident in Puerto Vallarta. Sky was a dedicated, hard-working artist, trying to pay off the un-paid bills her husband had left when he stuck a gun to his head one morning up in Denver. Hard-working soul that she was, she also loved a party. Her grandkids called her Granny Go-Go.

One evening she said, "Come on! Let's go up to Dirty Old Cal's. There's always somebody interesting there."

Sky had a rickety old Volkswagen and we chugged up the mountainside as far as we could, parked the car, and climbed over boulders, stepped high over rivulets of I-don't-want-to-think-about-what, and sleeping dogs until we reached a flight of stairs going on up to his Hillside Manor.

It was an open-bar get together. That meant the bar was open; not necessarily stocked. No *botanas* were served, not even a peanut or a potato chip. But the place was packed with people.

The guests didn't seem to mind the lack of refreshments. There was much milling about, introductions, chatting and smoking. This was at a time before my pot-smoking days. I wouldn't even have recognized the distinctive odor of marijuana then. They could've been smoking Phillip Morris or the finest joint from Colombian, for all I knew. Everybody seemed happy.

Jungle Jean took me on a tour of this weird house with so many weird people in it. One thing that stuck in my memory was a hanging mattress in one of the bedrooms.

The single-bed mattress was laid on a frame of bamboo sticks. A heavy rope was tied to each corner of the frame. The ropes were threaded up to a pulley attached to the overhead ceiling. A guide rope hung from the pulley so that you could hoist the bed higher or lower it to the floor. This contraption hung in front of a big wide window, which looked out on to the bay. A *pabellon,* made of white mosquito netting was draped around the bed.

Jungle Jean explained that Dirty Old Cal liked to take his siestas swaying in the open breeze, but he didn't like mosquitoes zinging in his ear, and he was terrified of scorpions. I knew the mosquito netting could keep out most of the mosquitoes, but I thought scorpions could climb up the rope.

Suddenly the sound of singing over-powered the laughing, chatting voices of the folks in the house. We were drawn back outside by magic. The night sky was dotted with millions of twinkling stars. Fishing boats were anchored in the bay, and the waves bobbed their lights up and down, making them look like fireflies.

A barrel-chested, portly Italian stood there. Arms flung to the wind, he belted out into the night with a melodious baritone, "FIGORO! FIGORO! EH, FIGORO UN! FIGORO DO!"

We could have been in the greatest opera shell in the world or on a hillside in Puerto Vallarta. It really didn't matter.

One morning, when I walked into the Consular Agency, Dr. Jorge Ruiz was waiting for me. Dr. Ruiz had been selected by the Canadian Embassy as the official medic for any Canadian who needed medical treatment. We Americans took whoever was available, and were happy to have them on our side.

Dr. Ruiz told me about an American man living on the mountainside all alone, who had recently fallen and cracked his sacroiliac. This wasn't a gesso case, but he did need some care, and he didn't have anybody to rely upon. His name was Melvin Calthorpe.

The name didn't really ring a bell with me. Dr. Ruiz gave me the man's address and I promised to go see what I could do.

I drove as near as I could. A tunnel was being built through the mountain on which the house stood. The bulldozers had left his house standing almost on a pinnacle. A path led to the door, but there was a great abyss on three sides of the house. I feared that if they ever set off a stick of dynamite to blast for more tunneling, the house would end up in the ravine.

As I made my way up the hill and into Calthorpe's house, I had that déjà vu´ feeling that I had been here before, at night.

I climbed up to what had once been called The Manor of the Hillside. The door was open and I went in.

There were dried sticks in magnificent flower pots, which had once held luscious green ferns and palm trees. Chickens and roosters walked freely around what I remembered being a hospitable entertaining area, but you must remember, the one and only other time I was there was at night, and there was a lot of pot-smoking and singing going on. Maybe it hadn't been so pretty back then, after all.

Cal was pretty close to being Destitute.

We talked for a while and I found out he had a son whom he hadn't seen in over thirty years. Although he didn't consider himself estranged from him, he just hadn't seen him in a long time.

Cal was seventy-two years old at this time. He had worked as a draftsman for an engineering firm in Modesto, California, from which he received a pension of $300 dollars a month.

That small pension wouldn't take him very far. He had spent his savings back when he and Jungle Jean were together. She had disappeared long ago. He couldn't afford a maid, a cook, or a house-boy to help him.

This house had originally been built with servants' quarters at the lower gate. Cal had allowed a young couple and their baby to live there. Roberto was a cook in one of the restaurants in town, and he brought home left-over food for his family and Cal.

Roberto also ran important errands for Cal, such as picking up necessary items from the drug store, checking the post office, but most importantly, kept him supplied with El Presidente brandy.

Cal was using his tea cart as a walker, and it worked out perfectly for him. He could push it around the terrace and sit wherever he wanted. He could push it into the kitchen to make coffee or take food from the refrigerator. Despite his cracked back-side, he could navigate pretty well inside his house.

I never saw the tea cart without a dirty coffee cup, or the bottle of brandy sitting on it.

When I asked him why he had never applied for Social Security benefits, he said, "I never investigated that. I didn't figure they would pay me anything here in Mexico."

I told him, "It may take a while, and I don't know if I can do anything, but let me see."

He tea-carted me to his locked filing cabinet, and we began plowing through manila folders that had seen many rainy summers in Puerto Vallarta. Some of the documents were green with mold, and some had stuck together, but they were legible.

As I was gathering documents I thought might be helpful, getting ready for my crawl back down the hill, he stopped me, "Say, did you know I was a play-writer?" he asked.

"No, Cal, I didn't know that."

"Take this along and read it when you get the chance." He handed me a thick folder which had printed on the front, "My Six Loves".

What you should know is that every American Embassy and every American Consulate General in the world has a Federal Benefits Unit. This has nothing to do with the State Department. They share office building space for convenience, nothing more. One doesn't have any jurisdiction over the other.

Sometimes there is interaction between Federal Benefits and the American Citizen's Service of the embassies or consulates. Usually it is when one department wants a favor from the other department. You know that Scratch My Back type favor. Federal Benefits might request, through American Citizen's Service, that a consular agent do some investigative foot-work in the field for them, but as a rule, you as an American, can't do anything about your Federal Benefits business in a Consular Agency.

I had no hopes of succeeding in what I was about to attempt, but thought it worth the try.

Geraldine Llewallen de Cortez was the Chief of FBU at that time. Gerry and I had become friends over the years and I thought she might help.

I told her about Calthorpe's financial and health problems, and that I wanted to file for Social Security benefits on his behalf. That was never done!

Gerry explained how complicated the application forms were, and that she or one of her workers in FBU would have to interview the applicant personally; none of them could come to Puerto Vallarta. He would have to come to them.

"But, Gerry, this man can't even get out of his house. If it were burning down, we'd have to carry him on out on a gurney! Come on! Break a rule! Give me a chance at this!" I begged her.

It took some time, a lot of talking, and numerous phone calls, but we finally did it.

Cal didn't have a telephone, so each time I needed more information or his signature, I'd have to climb the hill again. Every time I'd visit him, he'd ask, "Have you read my play yet?"

"No, Cal, I just haven't had time, but I will." I promised.

On one of these visits I did a double-take when I saw a nude woman stretched out on a chaise lounge sunbathing. I'm sure my eyes popped and I quizzed him in an undertone, "Cripes! Who in the hell is that?"

Smugly, he said, "That's my roommate. Want to meet her?"

I shook my head. "No, I don't think so."

"Come over and take a look. She's very pretty." he taunted me. On closer look I discovered it was a life-size rubber mannequin!

"Oh my lord, Cal! Wherever did you get such a thing?"

"Mail order magazine." he answered, grinning from ear to ear. "She's anatomically correct too." he added. Dirty sick old man!

One afternoon, I did have the time so I pulled out his play, "My Six Loves", and began to read.

If nothing else, Cal had imagination and I learned one of the reasons why he was called Dirty Old Cal.

There was only one woman in the play, but she acted out six different roles. We've all heard this before, but he actually wrote it on paper. Number One Love was the epitome of gracious femininity. She was the perfect hostess for his home entertaining, and complemented him when he was required to attend outside social functions. When he tired of Number One, she changed wigs and slipped into the role of Number Two.

There was The Whore, His Best Friend's Wife, The Preacher's Wife, The Fifteen Year Old Girl … and finally, The Twelve Year Old Boy. I was sick to my stomach of dirty old men, but I wasn't through yet.

Griswold Rossmoor became my albatross. He more than qualified for the DOM title. He was dirty, old, and pretty close to being a Destitute.

Gris was a Princeton graduate and had been an architect in San Francisco before retiring to Puerto Vallarta in 1970.

Both he and his wife, Marsha, were tall handsome people. There was an aura of stateliness about them when they walked into a room. They often modeled for Nelly in her style shows when she was showing off those beautifully embroidered dresses, blouses, and shirts. Wow! That was a long time ago, wasn't it, Nelly de Barquet? If we couldn't afford one of Josefa's designs, we had to have Nelly's. Some could afford both.

In 1975 a group of us packed our suitcases and headed to San Miguel de Allende, Guanajuato, to study Spanish in the Instituto Allende. We invited Marsha and Gris to visit us

Marsha was sick before she left Puerto Vallarta. She was listless; she had neither energy, nor appetite in San Miguel. While they were with us we celebrated their fortieth wedding anniversary. Before they left I suggested she stop in Guadalajara to see a doctor before returning to Puerto Vallarta, where qualified doctors were almost non-existent in those days.

Marsha was indeed a sick woman. She had amoebic cysts in her liver. Many of us pleaded with Gris to take her back to California, but he claimed he couldn't afford it. Gris had a wealthy Aunt Marsha, or so he told us on many occasions. Fran Tremear was one of Marsha's closest friends, and she begged him to call his Aunt Marsha. He refused.

Marsha never left the hospital alive. She died on December 10, 1975. It was a cold drizzly day in Puerto Vallarta. All of us were so angry with Gris that we didn't want to go to Marsha's funeral, but we did.

Aunt Marsha didn't hang around too much longer either. When she died, Gris inherited her wealth. He decided to travel around the world. I never knew where he went, but somewhere along the way he met Doris, an alcoholic living in Hawaii. Doris became his second wife.

He brought her back to Puerto Vallarta and tried to fill the vacant space Marsha had left. It didn't work. Later he told me they had divorced, moved back to the States, got back together again, and remarried. It didn't work that time either.

Gris became a regular sight on Los Muertos Beach again. His favorite hang-out was El Dorado Restaurant. I don't know what he was doing for money in those days, but he wasn't paying his bar bill. He was an absolute nuisance to anybody else who went to that restaurant. He was always trying to cadge drinks and lunch off anybody he recognized. He became worse and worse.

One day an old friend from San Francisco was in town and took notice of what was going on. The friend paid off his tab at El Dorado. The manager told Gris he was no longer welcome there.

I knew Gris and Marsha had two good-for-nothing daughters who had been Flower Children in the '60's. Penny lived in London with her husband and twelve year old son. Debbie lived in the Bay area of California.

I wrote what I thought was an anonymous letter to Debbie. I described Gris' living conditions, and told her I thought it was about time she or her sister took some action. I signed it, A Friend of the Family.

Debbie came, spent a few days with Gris, and then took him back with her to a commune in New Mexico where she was living.

That arrangement didn't work out to be satisfactory at all. The commune was a farm fourteen miles from the nearest town. Gris was too old to work like the younger men, but he stayed in the bunk house with them. He claimed he couldn't sleep for their loud card games and the cigarette smoke in the room. Debbie moved to San Francisco with her guru, leaving Daddy behind.

The commune over-boss called me one day, and said Gris wanted to come back. I felt like I had been punched in the belly. The last thing I wanted to see was Gris Rossmoor back in Puerto Vallarta.

I explained to the caller how life had been for Gris the last time he was here. I told her he had no friends, no family, nor anybody to look out for him. I learned from her that life wasn't too good for him there either. I asked her to try talking him out of this notion to return.

Not many days passed before she called again. Gris was determined to return. I asked the commune lady about his finances. She told me he didn't owe her anything, and that daughter Debbie had been responsible for his expenses.

Ump! Another low blow to the belly!

I knew Gris had to be receiving around $600 dollars from Social Security. Surely, he had other income. This man was sad, he was lonely, he missed his beach, but he couldn't be another Destitute!

Ginger, I believe her name was, and I talked for hours about Gris' predicament. He would be living on slim rations, but if she could get him here with two months Social Security payments, we figured we could handle him.

Dear Luis Guillermo and I put our heads together. We didn't have many options, but we settled on Los Tabachines, once again, as a safe haven.

Gris would be arriving on Sunday afternoon. Reservations had been made at Los Tabachines. Commune Ginger had worked miracles. Looking back on what transpired, she must have passed the hat around the commune, maybe even around the community.

He arrived by Mexicana airlines with a small carry-on valise, a cashier's check of $1500 hundred dollars, and few dollars in cash. Commune Ginger had written the name and address of Los Tabachines on a card for him to give to the taxi driver at the airport. Luis Guillermo would check in on him later in the afternoon.

How he managed to get this far on his own, I'll never know. He knew people around town, so it was easy for him to cash the check. He paid $300 dollars for one month rent in advance. He went to the immigration office and renewed his old resident status, and paid for that. Then he opened a bank account with $1,000 dollars. Sounds good, doesn't it?

Within two weeks he was at the Consular Agency. The bank cancelled his check book because he had emptied his account almost before it was opened. He had scribbled notes to himself all over his immigration book, and had even cut some pages out of it. He was broke and he needed food money.

I knew he had a check coming so I advanced him enough to live on for the week. Los Tabachines' dining room never was good, but now it was worse than in Perry Graystone's days.

Three more weeks rolled by and Gris still didn't receive a check. I knew this because Ginger and I had arranged for all his mail to be forwarded to the Consular Agency. No letter arrived.

Ginger gave me Debbie's phone number in San Francisco. She and her guru were living in a house trailer parked in a friend's back yard. When I finally reached her, and explained what the situation was, she said, "Well, I'll send him some of his Social Security money."

"What do you mean? You'll send him some of his Social Security money?" I asked, almost in disbelief at what I had heard.

She explained that when she left New Mexico, she had written to the Social Security office, and changed his address to her own in San Francisco. This way, she 'could monitor his needs'.

I said to her, in a very low, moderated, meaningful voice, "Debbie, if I don't have that full check in my hands within fifteen days, allowing for the slowness of Burro Express, your father's cause of death will read, Daughter Starved Him.

"But what am I going to live on?" she whined.

"The grub worms that live under the same rotten log you do", I retorted.

I called the Social Security office in Wilkes Barre, Pennsylvania and told them I was the consular agent in Puerto Vallarta. I pleaded Gris' case with the man who answered the phone. I told him that I had a Power of Attorney in my hand, signed by Gris, giving me the authority to receive his Social Security check in the Consular Agency, and that I would Fax him a copy immediately. I asked him, due to the circumstances, to forego the normal three-month wait for an address change. You see how easy fraud is, don't you?

Of course, I didn't have anything signed by Gris, but within thirty minutes I did, and it was sent by Fax to Pennsylvania. I hope nobody in the State Department ever reads this book. They would change the infallible Foreign Affairs Manuals to prevent this kind of manipulating documents.

However sympathetic the bureaucrap up in Wilkes Barre might have been, it took the usual three months for Gris' checks to start coming in. Debbie never sent money. I was able to stall the owners of Los Tabachines for another month, and I kept doling out money to him from my own pocket. Each time he borrowed money, he signed what we named The Gris Book. He wrote in the date and amount he received. The total amount was never overwhelming. Maybe he was still hitting on his old friends for a sandwich or beer, I really don't know.

Before we got too deeply in debt, a man and woman came knocking on our garden door one Saturday afternoon. Howard answered, and I could hear the man say, "I've come to see The Angel!" As Howard led them up the steps to our living quarters, I could hear this man keep saying, "I'm looking for The Angel. I'm looking for The Angel!"

Gris' Grand Benefactor had arrived. This tall, loud talking, blustering man had the biggest set of wings on his shoulders I had ever seen.

He introduced his traveling companion, Marty, who owned a nursing home in California. They had run into Gris and he told them the trouble he was having. This is the same guy who paid the bar bill at El Dorado many months ago.

He asked that his name never be divulged, nor the organization which he represented. I still honor that.

Benefactor was a California entrepreneur. He owned office buildings, apartment buildings, and a plant nursery in Dana Point. He also owned a ranch in Las Arandas, *Jalisco*, which is known as Los Altos de *Jalisco*, meaning The Highlands of *Jalisco*.

He was a member of a men's retirement group in California. This group was not affiliated with religion, politics, or any front-running organization. It was simply a group of men who had been successful in their businesses, and now wanted to help others. They met once a month in a private clubroom in a swank San Francisco hotel. Some of these men had known Gris in his younger years. They came to the rescue.

Big Wings wrote me a check for $400 dollars, and told me, "You'll get the same amount every month as long as he needs it."

We kept a close record of monies spent from this account. Luis Guillermo and I opened a bank account in Gris' name, but Gris couldn't write checks on it. Any check written could be signed by Jackie or Luis Guillermo, but to be valid, it had to carry my signature as well.

I paid Los Tabachines $200 dollars, and signed a Promissory Note to pay the balance as we could. That left him about $7 dollars a day to live on. I explained to Gris that until his Social Security checks started coming in, he would be on a very strict budget.

We set up a routine where Gris would come to the Consular Agency every Friday morning and draw out about $50 dollars for the coming week's expenses. Luis Guillermo made a photo copy of the ledger sheet from The Gris Book each time he gave him money. He always wanted to know what his balance was. Who could blame him? He just couldn't remember from week to week whether he had $10 dollars or $500 dollars.

He was growing very unhappy and grouchy. The staff at Los Tabachines was growing unhappy with him also.

As long as I had known Gris, even when Marsha was alive, he had his up days and his bottom days, depending on the season, I guess. On his up days he had a boob fixation. He would cut out pictures of pretty girls in bikini bathing suits with over-flowing Hooters and paste them around his bathroom mirror. On his bottom days, he would change the décor and paste pictures of full-hipped bathing beauties where the boobs had been. You've got me. I'm not the shrink.

The problem with Gris' up and bottom fixations was that they became more than just cut-outs on the wall. He wanted to fondle the uppers, and pinch or pat the bottoms. The female staff at Los Tabachines didn't like that. To them, he was just a Dirty Old Man.

Gris made friends with a male nurse at Los Tabachines. Ricardo had an apartment attached to his house in El Pitiallal, a suburb of Puerto Vallarta, and he was willing to have Gris live there for the same amount of money he was paying to Los Tabachines. He knew what the financial situation was and he understood that he wouldn't get paid anything at all until the California check or the Social Security check arrived. Los Tabachines manager was delighted with this arrangement. He had my Promise to Pay Note, and he was getting rid of a bad customer. Gris moved to El Pitiallal.

We were now going into the second month of this day-to-day, hand-to-mouth living. True to Big Wings' word, the California check arrived near the first of the month. We continued with the same routine. $100 dollars went to Los Tabachines, $100 went to the male nurse, and $200 was doled out on a weekly basis to Gris. None of this made him any happier.

I went once to visit him, and it had been a mistake for him to move. His apartment was spacious enough and adequately furnished; Ricardo's wife was fixing meals for him, and washing his clothes. But the apartment was above the nurse's garage, and about six long blocks to the nearest bus stop. I promised him we would look for another place as soon as we had some money to work with.

Damn Debbie for being the lazy, thieving, good-for-nothing daughter that she was! Damn the Bureaucraps in the Social Security offices all over the world!

We started the third month out with another $400 dollars from the Big Wings Club. This time the nurse got $200 and we kept $200 for Gris. The Friday visits continued. He was really trying to be patient, but he wanted a change, and so did Jackie, Luis Guillermo, and I.

I called the Social Security office at the Consulate "Can't you do anything?" I asked. "This man shouldn't have to live like this!" I was told that I should have patience. Have Patience? Patience, my ass!

Rule Number ONE. Never, but never, insult a Bureaucrap in a Social Security office. If you do, your file goes to the bottom drawer under all of those others who have insulted them. Incidentally, that same rule applies in all immigration and customs offices, in fact, in almost all federal government offices.

After much screaming, burning of telephone lines, and help from California Benefactors, we finally got Gris into what was a comfortable money-flow situation. Time to move.

Angelo Galeana, husband of Judy, knew his neighborhood well. He saw a *Se Renta* sign near their house. It was a sparsely furnished one-bedroom apartment, but it was ideally located. The land-lady, Doña Teri, ran a lunch counter next door; it was within walking distance of the beach, several bars and restaurants, and two blocks from the nearest hospital. Doña Teri's daughter, Gigi, was willing to keep Gris and the place clean for a price. The price was right. We jumped for it!

We worked out a routine where Luis Guillermo would visit him every Friday, pay Gigi for the week, and Doña Teri for meals he might have eaten in her place. He usually ate breakfast there, and signed a tab. His pocket money allowance was about $85 dollars a week. His needs were few. He never bought a bar of soap, or a roll of toilet paper. I don't think he used deodorant, and he certainly never needed a new razor blade. Gigi took good care of him. His main entertainment was going to a movie ... a pornographic one preferably.

For the first time in his life, probably, he was spending less than his income. We had kept his California Benefactor account on a separate ledger sheet from The Gris Book. He now had close to $2,000 dollars to fall back on in case of emergency.

I called Mr. Big Wings in Dana Point and told him I believed we could get along without the monthly check now. There might be a greater need some where else. He was amazed at how solid his friend had become. He offered Luis Guillermo and me a job to come work for him. I don't know about Luis Guillermo, but not accepting his job offer was probably the third biggest mistake I ever made in my life.

Nancy and Tony were winter residents who occupied the apartment next door to Gris. She took him under her wings. She cut his hair, trimmed his long growing white beard and. invited him over for dinner often

For some time I had been trying to convince him he should carry a walking stick. He adamantly refused. He wasn't very steady on his feet and Puerto Vallarta's quaint cobblestone streets can be treacherous. He toddled down to the corner every evening for his cocktail at the Toucan or El Torito Bars. I was afraid he might stumble and fall.

Christmas was right around the corner. I suggested to Gris he might want to buy Gigi and her mother a little gift, and take a nice bottle of wine to Nancy and Tony. He agreed that would be nice, but he wanted to send his daughters and grandson some money.

I've never been a parent so I don't recognize what I would call pangs of guilt, but I do love to wrap presents at Christmastime. We argued. I told him they were good-for-nothing kids; they never sent him even a note, and they didn't deserve a gift from him. He shut me up when he reminded me, "Well, it is my money, you know."

I bought a box of candy for Gigi, a potted plant for Doña Teri. I bought the bottle of wine, and I wrote three $15 dollar checks. I also told him it was about time he had some new clothes. We argued again.

He had brought a small valise with him to Mexico, but it was mainly stuffed with photographs of him, Marsha, and the two girls. He had a change of clothes, and that was it. This time I won.

After buying clothes, gifts, and sending those checks off, Gris still was within the budget. Luis Guillermo and I decided that since it was Christmastime, maybe he should have a bit more rattling money in his pocket. After all, his comrades at the corner bars had been good to him. If he had had one too many, they would help him across the street, and point him in the right direction back to his apartment. How much does a beer cost? We had worked hard to get where we were. We decided Gris should have an extra $50 dollars to blow and piss off however he wanted. Big deal! That would maybe buy fifty beers and he would still have eating money.

The day after Christmas Gris called. He was broke. Luis Guillermo pulled money from the account and went to see him. Gris had not bought drinks for his friends in his favorite bar. He'd seen a Hooter in The Toucan, and invited her home with him.

Luis Guillermo was bent double with laughter when he returned to the office to relate what had happened to Gris' money.

She was what she was, but didn't seem to have many moral codes. She stretched her arms high, pulled off her blouse, and Gris went for his Hooter Day. While he was gumming her, she deftly reached behind him where he had stashed his Christmas dollars, and tucked them into her panties. As soon as the Upper Portion was over, she wiped off her boobs, put on her blouse, and went on her way. Only then did Gris discover he had been left to spend Christmas day without money.

Gris was truly incorrigible, but he was the former husband of my friend, Marsha.

My Christmas gift for him that year was a Talpa walking stick. These are made from the root of a bamboo plant. They are famous in this part of the country. The root of the plant becomes the handle of the stick. It has three short prongs which make it look like an animal head. Some people call them *burros,* although I don't think they resemble a donkey.

My fly-friend Olga and I had been in Talpa a few weeks earlier and I bought the stick for Gris. I took it to the shoemaker who made a rubber tip for it that looked like a tiny huarache. Olga and I sat on the terrace of one of those old rambling ranch houses and decorated the walking stick. She painted green holly leaves and red berries up and down the stick. On one side I wrote, "In Case Of Emergency, Call 2-25-69."

As stubborn as he had originally been about using a walking stick, he loved it. The waiters in the bars didn't. With the cane part in his hand, he would reach out with the handle part and catch them by the leg. Sorry, boys, but I'm glad I bought it for him.

Dr. Francisco Gonzales was a friend of Doña Teri's son. He often stopped by her lunch counter for a snack. Over the years he had gotten to know Gris, and looked after his minor ailments. One night about ten o'clock, Dr. Pancho called to tell me Gris had fallen and broken his hip. He had found my home number on the walking stick.

Gris never walked again.

We placed a black ribbon on the office door the day of his funeral. We left Jackie to handle emergency calls. Luis Guillermo and I joined, Dr. Pancho, Gigi, Doña Teri, Nancy, Tony, the two daughters, Penny and Debbie for his mass.

There was a visiting priest from Seattle in town. He asked us to sit in chairs placed in a semi-circle in front of the altar. All of us were invited to share our life experiences with Gris, if we wished.

I didn't tell everything, but I talked about Marsha and Gris' fortieth wedding anniversary twenty years back.

After the hospital and doctors' bills were paid, there was about $500 dollars left in his account. He had two weeks paid up rent left. I told the daughters if they could live on that amount for the two weeks, they might as well stay on and enjoy Gris' legacy to them.

CHAPTER FOURTEEN

Pistol Packing

February 7, 1985 changed the lives of many people forever. I don't know if Enrique Camarena, Sr. was packin' that day or not, but if he was, he never got the chance to use it.

Camarena was abducted outside the Consulate General in Guadalajara, along with his pilot, as he was about to get in his truck and drive off to meet his wife for lunch. Their mutilated and tortured bodies were not found until about a month later.

The Drug Enforcement Agency had maintained presence at our Embassy and Consulate Generals throughout Mexico for several years. Agent Camarena's death was a blow to DEA and everybody else who knew Kiki.

Besides DEA attaches, we also had FeeBees. Those are Federal Bureau Investigation officers. Officially, they were called Regional Security Officers, but the Mexicans called them FeeBees. Security and personnel protection should be high on the list these days, but it was just coming into vogue for lowly consular agents in the eighties.

Our homes and offices were inspected and security enhanced. We had alarm systems installed in our home, but not at the office. The office door and the front door of our house were equipped with special issue locks. Each lock came with two keys, and if you needed more keys you had to get a special issue permit from FBI in Washington, D.C. We no longer had uncontrolled direct contact with anybody entering the Consular Agencies. What looked to be bullet-proof glass was installed above our work counter to separate us from the public. Secret is that it was nothing but heavy-duty plastic. I still use a left-over piece as my kitchen cutting board. All outside windows were covered with Mylar.

The local police department had sent me Rafael Ventura, a daytime security guard, long before the State Department decided we might need extra protection. Rafael was a handsome man with a pleasant, but serious face. He was very polite; he could smile if he had to, and he knew just how many paces to stay behind me when we were walking into a building. If I had to attend a local conference, or appear at a breakfast meeting, he stood off in a corner where he could see me, but not be seen by too many others.

He is the only Mexican I ever knew whose face turned black, and I do mean black, when he got angry. One day we were on our way to Nuevo Vallarta, a toney residential subdivision north of the airport, when a bus driver pulled over into our lane at a stop sign.

Without a word, Rafael turned off the ignition switch, grabbed his black pouch where he kept his gun, yanked the car door open and got out. He walked over to the bus driver's side. I don't know what he said to him, but when he got back in the car, his face was black as black could be.

He growled, "That's one that'll never pull out in front of this green car again!" I just sat there, thankful that he had kept his black pouch zipped.

I don't know what was expected of me after work hours, but each morning I went to work, Rafael was waiting for me outside the front door of my house. We walked to work together, and he walked me home in the afternoons, but I was allowed to go the bathroom by myself.

Rafael was an excellent driver. He had worked as a long-haul truck driver before joining the police force. At times, he would run errands for me in my car, such as delivering letters and forms to other offices, or delivering items to jail.

Then somebody up in D.C. decided we'd better have guns!

We've always had guns in my family. I don't know if anybody ever used one, but you never knew when a stray rabid dog might come down the road. I never fired a gun and never wanted to do so. I didn't want a gun, and I didn't want to learn to shoot it, but I was issued a .38 S&W, and told, "Go to the practice range as often as you can."

Practice range? Puerto Vallarta didn't have one! Foreigners weren't even supposed to have arms in their possession, and here I was with a .38 sitting in my lap!

One day I mentioned my predicament to Admiral Ortega. He told me, "Not to worry, *muchacha,* I'll send you out with the best artillery officer I have on base. He'll have you shooting in no time."

I would drive out to the Naval Zone every time I had some free time. His officer, driver and I would go in the Admiral's car to a vacant field and practice. We used paper bull's eye charts as our target. The driver would thumb tack one to a fence post, and I fired from about thirty feet away. The first day I must have used a whole box of ammo, and the best I could do was clip a corners off the chart. The officer thought my gun must be misaligned. Nobody could miss the whole damn chart like I was doing!

But I was persistent and the officer was patient. After each time we went for a shoot, we would take my charts back to the Admiral. He would slowly shake his head, and look questionably at his officer. The officer stood at attention.

I would walk around in the daytime curling my index finger, pretending I was pulling the trigger. At night I would dream of those bull's eye charts filled with bullet holes. Then one day my dream came true.

When we presented my charts to the Admiral on that day, he laughed and said, "I suggest you mount this chart permanently on your front door. You'll never be bothered by anybody."

We've always heard, "Practice makes perfect." So? I was perfect and didn't need to practice. Besides, I had Lieutenant Mario at night, Rafael in the daytime, and Howard on week-ends. All three of them were experts in gunmanship, so I didn't need to practice.

Foreign Service officers at embassies and consulates are shuffled constantly. Most are reassigned every eighteen to twenty-four months. This policy does not apply to consular agents. We were hired because we were already in place.

The FeeBee Regional Security officer in Guadalajara was re-posted and a new one took his place.

Erwin Wallace called to tell me what day he would be in town, and he wanted to arrange a target practice session. He suggested I invite Chief of Police Miguel Angel Villanueva to come along.

I should have kept up my practice. I literally trembled at the thought of target practice with an FBI agent. But it was part of the job.

Howard was flying in from Houston and Wallace was flying from Guadalajara. I met them both at the airport. Howard had the weekly border-order of Owen's breakfast sausage, sirloin steaks, and Roquefort cheese in his carry-on. Of course, that's not allowed. It's against Customs Regulations. That's called *fayuca* in Spanish, but he was well-known by Puerto Vallarta Aduana agents, and he usually was bringing in their requests also.

Wallace's luggage was the usual dark carry-on plus an iron-clad box holding about a hundred pounds of different gauge and size bullets and shells. He carried his pistol, shot-gun and rifle in a duffle bag over his shoulder. Can you imagine getting on a plane like that these days!

We spent the rest of the afternoon shooting blanks from one end of our terrace to the other. He brought me a scabbard which my .38 fit in very nicely. I had that scabbard belted around my waist and tied down to my thigh, just like Dale Evans and Annie Oakley.

The procedure was to: "Pull, Aim, Fire, Fire, Re-holster!"

"Pull!" I pulled my gun. "Aim!" I aimed. Sometimes he would try to trip me up and yelled, "Fire! Fire! Fire!" instead of two times.

Finally, he said. "We'd better rest now. Your finger won't be worth a damn tomorrow." He also showed us a few close contact defense maneuvers. I already knew one of them.

Nine o'clock came early the next morning. Wallace had spent the night at our house, so we were ready to go when Rafael came for us. We had left the heavy ammo in our locked car in the locked garage the night before. We drove by the police station; Chief Villanueva, and several of his officers pulled ahead of us to direct us to Piruli's ranch where we would be target practicing.

Piruli was a popular singer in Mexico in the eighties, but an angry, maybe jealous, gunman cut him down on the front steps at his own home in Mexico City. That ranch was sold long ago, and is now becoming a residential section.

Wallace's idea was to have me go first. Rafael would be next in line. Then if the Chief or any of the other officers wanted to take a try, he would furnish the ammo. He must have received a handsome ammunition allowance when he left Washington, D.C. He brought most of it to Puerto Vallarta.

There were no blanks in my gun today. My pistol was strapped to my leg and I was fearless. His targets differed from what I had used when I practiced with the Navy officer. His were made of paper also, but when unrolled, they showed a life-size bulky, ugly man coming at you with a drawn pistol in his hand.

"Take him out!" Wallace yelled. I pulled, aimed, fired twice and re-holstered, just as I had in practice the afternoon before. He yelled, "Why did you re-holster? He's still coming at you!"

I looked at the target; it only had one bullet hole in it, and that was in the shoulder of the arm that was not holding the gun.

"O.K. Let's try it again!" he said, as he stapled another ugly chart to a tree.

I pulled, aimed, fired four times and heard a sickening click. I had run out of bullets. He yelled, "Re-load, he's still coming at you!"

My hands were sweating, and my heart was pumping as I fumbled in my pocket for another clip and quickly re-loaded. I fired five more times at the approaching gunman. Suddenly, I heard a collective gasp from the police officers behind me and Wallace was staring at me with his mouth open.

I had not killed my would-be assailant, but I had stopped him. One got him just about at his belly-button; the other four followed a straight path down. I had passed my test, and it was now Rafael's turn.

All the excitement and eagerness seemed to have gone out of the crowd. The men fired off a few shots. Somebody picked up some soft drink bottles scattered around, and stacked them for the Chief to take a shot at. He missed them all.

Wallace left the unused ammunition with me, saying, "You may need to buy a favor with this sometime."

At times the city coffers ran dry, and the police department couldn't buy ammunition for the men. Rafael's and his buddies' guns were always loaded.

In all the years that gun was in my care, I never had to use it, thank Goodness. However, the burglar alarm installed in our house warned away three would-be burglars who didn't know about my shooting prowess.

CHAPTER FIFTEEN

Gays In The Tropics

Puerto Vallarta is now known to be gay-friendly, but that wasn't the case back in the early eighties. We now have bars, restaurants, hotels and B&B's that cater to homosexuals. In fact, the city's economy depends heavily on gay residents and tourists. But the gay life in Puerto Vallarta has a dark shadow as well.

I met Javier when he operated a tiny grocery store near Los Muertos Beach. We lived in that part of town at the time, and his store was convenient to pop in for a loaf of bread or some other last-minute item. His hot sweet potatoes baked in their skins were a special treat, and made a good mid-morning snack. Javier moved on from the grocery store to the Café Revolucion. That place had heavy traffic both day and night from an extremely diversified crowd. It was a handy place to stop in for a cold beer on the way home from the post office.

I knew a group of ladies who enjoyed a birthday luncheon there each month. There was a hole-in-the-wall drugstore across the street and my mean friend, Pat Flanery, would always treat us to an injection of B-12 when the partying was over.

Javier made a gift of Mexican enema cans to all his favorite female visitors. Those of you who have lived in Mexico for a long time may have seen one of these cans. If you haven't been properly introduced, you would never recognize one. It looks like a metal one-pound coffee can with a handle stuck on the side. Down toward the bottom is a spout, which has a long, skinny rubber hose attached to it. On the end of the hose is a nozzle. You could personalize the can any way you desired, but they remained on their special shelf in Cafe Revolucion. I decided it was time to drop out of the monthly celebrations when Pat wanted to paint the American flag on my can.

The morning the news broke that Javier had died the night before from multiple stab wounds shocked and saddened the townspeople of Puerto Vallarta.

Today there are tall trees overlooking a tiny lake on a ranch outside of Talpa de Allende, *Jalisco*. They were planted there in his memory.

Josh and Lane were residents who hailed from Texas. They built one of the first mansions in Mismaloya and entertained often and sumptuously. One night I received a call from one of the hospitals that Josh had been shot. I went. I knew he was in trouble when I heard his story. I doubt that we will ever know the truth of what actually happened there, but the fact was that Lane had taken a bullet through his heart as he lay in his own bed.

Josh said two Mexican men rang the doorbell and asked if they could come in. He offered to make them a cocktail. Then they asked to see Lane.

Josh told them he was downstairs and led the way to his bedroom. He claims both men fired bullets at Lane, and that he got in the way of two of them himself; one through the fleshy part of his waist and another nipped one of his fingers.

The two assailants fled in Josh and Lane's Safari, grabbing the keys hanging on a wall in the kitchen on their way out the front door. Before Josh could be arrested for any part the police might have thought he played in Lane's death, he was assisted in leaving the country for a Texas hospital.

Lane was from a wealthy family. His father hired his own investigation team in Texas to come down to find the culprits accountable for his son's death. They met with the police officials, and they met with me. The case was never solved, but the local police surmised that the perpetrators might have been uncles, fathers or older brothers of young boys who had been lured down a different path from theirs.

North Johnson, my Canadian counterpart in those days, had been invited to our house for Thanksgiving dinner. He called the morning of that Thanksgiving to tell me he would not be our guest that day. He was working the death case of his Canadian friend and neighbor, David, who had been stabbed to death in his home the night before. I insisted that he get his paperwork done, leave the gory details to the police and mortician, and come give thanks with us that he hadn't been visiting David when knife-toters came to call.

North had warned his friend many times to forget the young boys playing soccer on the beaches.

Semi-open homosexuality brought fear into the homes of many locals. It also brought AIDS and shame into some upstanding, outstanding homes. You have to remember that "safe sex" was not even a word down here at that time.

The United States recognized the existence and the need of education about gay activities long before some other countries. I remember going to a conference at the Embassy in Mexico City, and discovering that our own AID, Agency for International Development, had printed out beautiful posters, which were displayed on busses, subways, trains and in many public places in the United States.

I armed myself with all the posters I could carry and prepared to leave on an early morning flight to Puerto Vallarta. My intentions were to ask proprietors of local gay establishments to hang these posters in their restrooms. The prettiest one of all was of two handsome young men standing close together, one holding out a hand containing a condom to his friend. The caption read…"because I care for you…" That poster was stolen from my hotel room. Maybe it sent the right message after all.

Dra. Irma Battleson phoned me about an AIDS case she had been treating. She told me he had no money to pay her; she was leaving on vacation, and would not be continuing with him when she returned. She said he had fallen and broken a couple of ribs. She gave me his name and address.

I went to see Jason, but nobody answered the door. He didn't have a phone, so I wrote a note on the back of one of my business cards and slipped it under the door. "If we can help you, let me know."

I never heard from him, but one day his neighbor came to see me. She said she had not seen him leave his house in several days.

She told me, "*Señora,* I know he's sick and I'm worried. There's an awful odor coming from his house."

The first thing I thought of was that he'd died. The first person I thought of was my favorite mortician.

I phoned Ignacio and asked, "Could you come go with me? We'll pick up the locksmith, Braulio Herrera, who is across the street from the Consular Agency, and go see what we find. I think he must be dead."

"No, no, Jenny. We can't do that! That's against the law! That's breaking and entering! Call the D.A. first."

Of course he was right. My hat was on backwards that day. I called the District Attorney's office. She was new in her office, but she knew her job well. She agreed we should investigate. She would pick up the locksmith and meet me at Jason's house soon. She brought along two of her state policemen also.

Again, nobody answered the knock on the door. The lock was picked in no time, and we went into a shadowy entryway. There was a small dipping pool inside. The walls were painted forest green, and the pool was tiled in the same color. You couldn't see the bottom of the murky pool, and at first we thought the water had turned into pond scum soup. The policemen shined their flashlights into the pool, but couldn't see any form resting on the bottom. However, there was a powerful stench of death in this house.

We slowly climbed the stairway leading to the second floor. I began to get a feeling of *dejà vu* that I had been in this house before when Patricia Rowan owned it, but that was many years ago, and the house had obviously been recently remodeled. The higher we climbed, the stronger the disgusting odor became.

The District Attorney, Erika Polifox, and I stood by an open window while her two policemen explored every room, opening and closing the doors as they went. The new owner of this house must have been planning to operate it as a hotel because each room down the hallway was a bedroom.

At last one of the policemen shouted, "I found him! He's in here!" He walked back to the window where we were standing and told his boss, "He's in there alright. He's in bed. *Jefa*, it may be my imagination, but I thought I saw him breathe. Whew! *Fuche!* He has no clothes on. You don't want to go in there!"

His boss, the *jefa* replied, "It may *fuche*, but this is my job." She pulled a handkerchief from her purse, held it to her nose, and walked toward the room at the end of the hall.

I thought to myself, "I can't let this woman do this alone. This is my job too, and after all, this is an American," so I called after her, "Wait for me! I'm coming with you." I sprayed my handkerchief with a germ killer, which I always carried in my handbag, and followed her down the hall.

There he was. Just as the policemen had described. He was in bed nude. He had a wide elastic bandage wrapped around his chest protecting his broken ribs, I assumed.

The district attorney and I stared down in astonishment at this man. She glanced over at me and whispered, "He's dead. Rigor mortis has already set in. Did you ever see anything like that in your life?" I admitted that, actually, I never had. She slowly shook her head and lamented, "Too bad he's dead."

We walked out of the room and back to the window where the smell was less nauseating. She contacted her office on her two-way radio, and asked her secretary to call Ignacio to come pick up the body. I suggested that we wait for him downstairs, and out on the street. The smell was less repulsive outside.

Ignacio was doing well in the body business. He drove up in a used, but acceptable real-life funeral hearse. His helpers unloaded the gurney, and all of us trudged back up the stairs. The gurney bearers went to the room where Jason's body lay, but returned shortly with a puzzled look on their faces. One said, "There's nobody in there!"

"Nobody in there? We just came out of that room! The man is dead! He couldn't have walked past us! We've been right here. Are you positive?"

"There's nobody in there, *Señora*," he assured me.

Polifox and I walked back down the hallway and into Jason's room. Sure enough, there was nobody in the room.

I called out, "Jason, Jason, are you here?" Nobody answered. I'd never dealt with a disappearing body before. I kept calling, "Jason! Jason! Are you in here?"

Suddenly, Jason stepped out of a door that none of us had noticed before. I don't know who was more shocked, the district attorney, Jason, or me. He stood there desperately trying to cover his Rigor Mortis with the elastic bandage.

I reached for the bed sheet, handed it to him, and told him to go sit on the bed.

First, I apologized for intruding upon his privacy, then I told him who we were and why we were there. The district attorney left the room, and Jason and I talked. I told him I knew he was sick, and that I would help if I could. He casually brushed my concern aside, saying, "It's only a couple of broken ribs." We talked about his need for food, and he assured me he was well in control of his needs. He had a friend who came by and brought him food occasionally. He didn't eat much.

I asked him, "Then tell me, Jason. What is that awful smell coming from this house that made all of us think you were dead?"

He shrugged his shoulders. "Hugo hasn't been by for several days to take the garbage out, and I haven't felt up to doing it myself."

About two weeks later Hugo reported to me that Jason had died in his sleep. Nobody ever mentioned the word AIDS.

One of my favorite recollections is of when I was invited to speak at a ladies' luncheon one day. This was back in early 1993 and Janet Reno had just been appointed by President Bill Clinton as the first woman Attorney General of the United States.

If you remember, in those days there was a big ruckus up in Washington regarding gays in the U. S. military. It was along about then the slogan was coined, "Don't ask. Don't tell."

I had totally forgotten about Mary Beth until she appeared at the Consular Agency one morning. Mary Beth had married a Catholic priest in the seventies, when men had first started leaving the church to marry. She and her husband had been big news on television. They moved to Yelapa and started their family. Daddy died from a venomous scorpion bite and Mary Beth had moved her brood back to the States.

Now she stood in the outer office explaining that she was ground coordinator for a cruise ship company, which would be bringing in a group of six hundred lesbian tourists for one day. She handed me her business card and pointed out the purple triangle, which indicated her customers' sexual preference.

I raised my eyebrows and asked her, "Mary Beth, have you changed your colors?" She laughed and said, "No, but there's money to be made in this field and I need the money."

Mary Beth had already made arrangements with *Señora* Ramal, the manager of Hotel Molina del Aqua, to have a luncheon in the hotel garden area by the swimming pool. She contacted Crystal Frost to have her interpretive dance group perform; she had Huichol Indians lined up to display some of their beaded art, and she had talked to Yolanda Franco, the Director of Tourism for the city. She wanted me to give a welcoming speech to the group.

She told me her group was made up of professionals from all walks of life. She thought it would be an interesting day, and I was free to invite any of my lady friends to come to the luncheon. I agreed to do my part.

Now, what would I talk about? I called one of the consuls in Guadalajara and explained what I had signed on for. She gave me the name of a woman at the State Department who was of tremendous help.

Armed with impressive statistics on how many women worked in the Foreign Service, how many served as ambassadors around the world, how many women congressmen served their country, the number of state governors who were women, how many were supreme court justices, plus Janet Reno's recent appointment, I thought I could make a pretty good talk.

I called a few friends, and after explaining what the day was all about, asked them to join me for lunch. Then I called Yolanda Franco, and asked what she would be speaking about at the luncheon. She informed me she had been ordered by her supervisors in Guadalajara to not attend. I didn't have that choice.

My invited group left our white gloves at home, but I thought we did dress appropriately to attend a 'gaaden paahty'. Wrong. Our gauzy, frilly Vallarta frocks were very much out of place.

We shared a delicious lunch with professional welders, plumbers, doctors, nurses, attorneys, truck drivers, and construction workers. As Mary Beth had said, '...from all walks of life.'

After lunch, several of the guests decided to take a dip in the swimming pool. Water overflowed out into the garden and over our pink polished toes.

Fortunately, all six hundred did not attend.

CHAPTER SIXTEEN

Disputes Re: Property

Property disputes took up an enormous amount of our time, and they usually were so futile. Every country has its' laws and policies, and we visitors should learn what they are and obey. We don't always comply.

A thick section of our FAMs is devoted to dealing with the rights of Americans in a foreign country. Most Americans don't read the entire sentence. They see it written like this: "I'm an Amuriken and I got rights!"

Up until 1973, a foreigner couldn't legally possess property in Mexico within fifty kilometers of the beach or a hundred kilometers from the border, but that didn't stop them from buying. There was an illegal loop-hole to do this, and it was called *prestanombre*. You found some Mexican you hoped you could trust, borrowed his name, bought the property and built your home. Fernando Romero, who designed and built many of the earlier homes in Gringo Gulch, was a trustworthy man, but he told me at one time he had thirty-five properties in his name, but only owned one.

Between 1911 and 1934 agrarian land reform returned confiscated land to millions of Mexican farmers who collectively received the land to work. This was called an *Ejido*. The members of the *Ejido* were *Ejidatarios*. In order to keep the land, they had to work it. They couldn't rent, lease, or sell it. They could pass it on to their heirs, but the heir had to do his share of the work also. This didn't always work properly either.

Sometimes an *Ejidatario* had a yearning for the green buck, and he convinced the ignorant gringo that he would sell him the piece of land he wanted for a good price. Money was exchanged for a signed paper on which might have been written The Lord's Prayer or tomorrow's grocery shopping list. The important thing was that it was signed. The foreigner would begin construction; the clan of the *Ejido* would tear it down or burn it down. Vandals! He'd start all over, and they would tear it down again. Sometimes this could get really nasty. Angry farmers tended to be very protective of their government-allotted land. This has happened all over Mexico.

In 1973 President Luis Echeverria Alvarez decreed that this *prestanombre* business was not going to continue. He came up with a law called The Foreign Investment Law which allowed foreigners to 'own in trust' within the restricted zone. You put your property in a Bank Trust account, and you paid an annual fee to the bank for managing your account. The bank held the title to your property.

We never had too many problems with this type of property ownership in Puerto Vallarta. Other parts of Mexico did. The trust management fees were set at the discretion of the bank. Some banks were a bit on the greedy side.

As always, there are some shady characters standing in the background looking for a way to take advantage of a law. One of these shady characters was the most likeable, charming man you would ever want to meet. Let's call him Raymundo, but that was not his name.

Foreigners were encouraged to come forward and regularize their property, and register as the true owner, in order to set up a bank trust account called *Fidecomiso*. At the same time Mexican property owners were threatened with the risk of having their property confiscated if they didn't pay their over-due land taxes. Raymundo enters.

He worked for the newly established *Fidecomiso* office. His job was to fly the aerial photographers over the city, so the surveyors could identify parcels of land.

The guys down at the *Fidecomiso* office were doing a really sloppy job of registering properties. When I think about it, I'm surprised more folks didn't try to do what Raymundo almost got away with doing.

Back then, anybody could pay land taxes on property, which didn't belong to them. Remember that the Mexican government was trying to collect back taxes. It didn't matter where the money came from. Pay the taxes, get a receipt, and it's yours.

Raymundo was privileged to inside information on who owed taxes and who didn't. A nice little piece of vacant land was sitting over there on Olas Altas Street, up the hill from Los Muertos Beach. The taxes were over-due. Raymundo paid them.

Foreigners were eager to invest in Puerto Vallarta in the early 70's. Interest rates in financial establishments were high. The country seemed politically and economically stable. We had not entered the fall-of-the- peso era yet. Construction of houses, condominiums, and apartment buildings became popular.

Raymundo sold his newly acquired property to Engineer Fernando Rivera.

Engineer Rivera immediately began building a two-story condominium building with six dwellings. They were an instant success; close to the popular beach, within easy walking distance of the best grocery store, drugstore, and movie theatre.

Five Canadians and one American bought these units. None were full-time residents, and usually occupied their condos only in the high season, that being wintertime.

People just don't walk away from a vacation house in Mexico, as you might do in the United States or Canada. Usually you have a maintenance maid or gardener to come in once or twice a week. There might even be a general manager to pay the domestics, and keep an eye on the place. In this case, Aurea Applegate had been left in charge. She and her husband, Ricardo, had been in property management for many years.

One summer night in the rainy season of 1989 the city police arrived at that building on Olas Altas. The police were accompanied by two huge moving vans, and while neighbors watched, the policemen broke the locks on all six residences with heavy hammers. The movers loaded their vans with furniture and all personal belongings of the owners, and hauled them away for storage.

Aurea phoned me the next day to tell me what had happened. She said she had been there during the ravaging, but there was nothing she could do to stop it. The original land owner's attorney had a judicial order to take possession of the building. Aurea suggested I might want to go to City Hall and talk with the syndic. I did.

"I've been working for fourteen years on this case," he told me, "and I've finally won!"

"But what is the case?" I asked. "All these people have their property in a Bank Trust! I thought that's what a foreigner had to do to be a legal owner! What now?"

"The man who built and sold them the condos didn't own the land he built on," he informed me.

"But what do these people do now? Is there no financial reimbursement for them?" I asked him.

"They could talk to the bank's trust officer, but the case is closed as far as I'm concerned. My client has won," he stated.

"So you're the attorney for the original owner of the land, and the city syndic also?"

"I was hired by the original owner many years before I became syndic for Puerto Vallarta," he advised me.

I left his office thinking, "That could've been us a few years ago." The condos that the Goldsmiths, the Glovers, Howard and I had bought, after our fiasco with Chico Lopez, were near the ones on Olas Altas. We had tried to register it with *Fidecomiso* in 1974, and were told that the rulings had not been made on condos yet. The Glovers and we sold, and moved on to other homes before the rulings came down.

Of course, this case had its share of press coverage. Pictures of burly policemen wielding sledge hammers in the rain made the front page of our local newspapers. These were picked up by Guadalajara press, and the news spread that another bunch of gringos had been ripped off.

A man came to see me, and introduced himself as Engineer Fernando Rivera. "Just the man I wanted to see," I'm thinking to myself, "but how am I going to handle this?"

I didn't have to. Engineer Rivera lived in Guadalajara, had read the news, and was appalled. He said, "I am an honest man, and I thought the man I bought the land from was also honest. The bank officer should never have accepted these accounts without a thorough investigation of the *escrituras,* the deeds. I'll take this to the highest courts in Mexico and I won't stop until I get a positive resolution to this problem."

I asked him if I could refer the inquiries I was getting from the foreigners to him.

"By all means," he reassured me, "but you'll be the first to know when I have my answer."

We shook hands and he promised to keep in touch with me. He left me with the feeling I had truly met an honest man. I didn't know how influential or powerful he might be in Guadalajara, but I knew that he wasn't a man to sit back and let his reputation be ruined.

Confederacion Trabajadores de Mexico, CTM, has put more men in Los Pinos presidential suite, kept more men out of there, kicked more foreigners out of their residences, boarded up and picketed more business establishments than you can shake a fist at.

Most foreigners didn't want to have anything to do with labor unions. The majority of us hired domestic help, and the first thing we asked them was, "Do you belong to the union?"

"No, *Señora*. No belong. Cost *mucho*. No help. No *sindicato*." It didn't make much difference if they belonged or not. If you fired one of your employees without giving them severance pay, even if they were lazy, or had stolen you blind, they could go to the union, and you ended up paying more than you would have had you followed the rules in the first place.

Phil Ober used to advise us to keep a logbook, which the employee would sign each time he was paid. This was a good idea for your own record keeping, but didn't necessarily satisfy the union bosses. Ron Walker, an American who has lived in Puerto Vallarta more years than I have, used to give lectures at foreign community gatherings regarding labor laws. Most of us complied with them. However, some workers were always on the look-out to make trouble for their *patrones*, the people who hired them.

I remember one case where a disgruntled house employee went to the local union and reported that her *patron* in Casa Mayo was renting his house to tourists. She felt that she and the other five employees were not getting a fair deal. Uhmuh!

Red banners were hung over the doors of the house. Nobody was allowed in or out. Casa Mayo's owner was cited to appear in the union's headquarters and pay an exorbitant fine. He wasn't even supposed to be renting out his house! That's making money! Immigration authorities got in on the act also. I was keeping close tabs on the development of this story in the local newspapers, but the American never contacted me.

One day I read that he had told his story to a Wall Street Journal reporter, and the Journal's article was published in the Vallarta Opina.

It read that Mr. Zane was a building contractor in Montana, and he often hosted his prospective clients to a complimentary visit in Casa Mayo, complete with one maid who did the cooking, and a gardener who cleaned and maintained the pool area. Mr. and Mrs. Zane also had a large family who enjoyed use of the house. The Zanes were about to lose their house to CTM because of one unhappy worker.

Robin Lloyd was a Welshman who moved to Puerto Vallarta from the US in the mid 80's. Robin also opted for US citizenship after he had piloted a PT boat for the US Navy in the Korean War. He was a writer for The Mexico City News and Guadalajara Colony Reporter, both English publications. He and Luis Reyes Brambila, of Vallarta Opina, became good friends, and Luis offered him the opportunity to re-establish the Vallarta Today, another English publication.

Robin would usually come by the Consular Agency right at closing time, and we would have long, interesting talks about everything, mostly about the political shenanigans in our town. Both of us were very interested in seeing how the Zane case would blow.

One day Robin said, "I just got word the Minister of Tourism is coming to town this week-end, and he might like to talk to you about how the Wall Street Journal is treating the Zane case. The Big Boys think it might hurt the tourist trade."

"Oh, Robin, I couldn't do that! He ought to talk to somebody at the Embassy. I don't have the authority to talk to the *Secretario de Turismo!* Whoever came up with that idea?"

"He did," Robin replied. "Why don't you invite us both for Sunday breakfast at your house? We'll just be the four of us. Listen to what he has to say."

There was nothing pretentious about this visit. Mr. Secretary knocked on our garden door at the appointed hour. Robin ran down the stairs to escort him up to our dining terrace. He didn't have a driver. He didn't have a body-guard. He had walked from City Hall to our house in The Gulch by himself.

Robin introduced us to the tall, white haired, bespectacled, handsome representative of the federal government. We shook hands and I said to him, "I'm honored to meet you, Mr. Secretary."

Still holding my hand, he said, "My name is Antonio Savignac. Call me Tony."

I could never make myself call him Tony, but we had a wonderful visit that morning. We talked about his schooling at Harvard, his family, his preference in vacation spots throughout the world, Mexico City in general, weather, restaurants, etc. We talked about everything except the Zanes.

When the time came to serve breakfast, I began to feel a little uneasy about what I had prepared. I make a fairly tasty biscuit; Howard had brought down our favorite Owen's sausage to go with scrambled eggs. I also planned to serve grits. Grits? With all his sophistication, this man probably didn't even know what grits were.

As I served the plates, I said to him, "*Señor*, this is something you probably have never eaten, but it's a Southern dish, which I hope you like. It's called grits."

The Minister of Tourism leaned back in his chair, slapped his leg, laughed, and said, "Jenny, I know grits. I used to drive a Mrs. Tucker's shortening truck throughout Tennessee and northern Mississippi in the summertime when I was going to school!"

There still had been no mention of the Zanes. I certainly didn't think it was my place to bring up the subject. I glanced at Robin and quickly raised my eyebrows. He smiled and slightly shrugged his shoulders. We may have spent another hour at the breakfast table. I thought, "Well, Robin, you got a free breakfast out of this, didn't you?"

As he was complimenting me on a good Southern breakfast, and we were saying goodbyes, he turned to me, almost as an after-thought, and asked, "What do you think we ought to do about Mr. Zane and his house?"

"Give it back to him," I answered.

And that is exactly what happened. Tourism is very important to Mexico.

Dope

We've had our share of dealing with druggies in Mexico. Why, some of the top officials have often been caught on the shady side of the law. For decades Mexico and the United States have struggled through strained relationships due to drug trafficking across the northern borders.

Some Big-Timers are now in prison, while others are still plying their trade successfully. I've always heard: As long as there's a market, the product will be furnished. It seems we haven't been able to dry up the market yet.

Mexico's military forces are its strongest weapon in the war against drugs. I've taken several Sunday cruises around our bay on luxurious, previously privately-owned vessels, which were confiscated by the Mexican Navy, simply for having the wrong cargo onboard.

From time to time there would be a *Quemadura* Oficial, usually at the Naval Zone. Army and Navy personnel, including other high-ranking federal authorities were invited to attend the Official Burn. I was always invited so I could report back to my supervising post, "Man, you ought to see what they're doing in Puerto Vallarta to fight marijuana growing! They're pulling it out of ground and burning it!"

A token amount of marijuana plants, supposedly from the tons that had been destroyed, were piled up on the esplanade, about fifty or sixty yards from the long table where we sat. An incinerator had been rigged to a device placed on the table in front of the military officer representing the branch that had been in charge of the harvesting. On signal, he pressed the button that ignited the plants, sending billowing black smoke into the air.

At one of these ceremonies I looked up and saw a flock of birds flying low over the cloud of smoke. I turned to the officer sitting next to me and asked, "What do you think will happen to those birds up there?"

"They'll die, but they'll die happy," he replied.

Another day I visited the Federal District Attorney's office about one of our locked up druggies. Obviously, I had chosen the wrong time to make this visit. These guys are all called *Licenciados*. Pronounce that: Lee-sen-see-ahdo. If you are truly on good terms with them, you address them as Lic. (Lick)

This particular Lic. welcomed me into his office, sat back down in his chair, pulled his shirt tail from his pants, unbuckled his belt, and unbuttoned the waistband of his pants. He leaned back in his big, leather executive chair, raised his arms up and locked his hands behind his head, then asked, "Now what can I do for you, *Señora?*"

It was six o'clock in the afternoon. More than likely, he had worked hard all day, taken a lunch break for a bowl of beans, and was back on the job; same as I.

He picked up a bowl sitting on his desk, and began picking through what looked like dried okra seed. I said to him, "Looks like you're getting ready to do a little gardening."

He sighed and said, "How I wish! I could soon retire. These are some of the finest seed I've ever seen."

"What are they?"

"Marijuana."

I've heard that when these soldiers find a growing field of marijuana, usually hidden in the cornfield growing up the side of a mountain, they pull up the stalk; vigorously shake the plant over the freshly turned soil to distribute some of the seeds for re-growth.

Rafael Caro Quintero, Ernesto Fonseca Carrillo, and Miguel Ángel Félix Gallardo were only a few of *Jalisco's* famous drug lords. Many of our city officials and leading businessmen were party rats with Ruben Zuno Arce, who is now living in Leavenworth, courtesy of the U.S. government.

I recall that when Zuno Arce's wife testified as a character witness for him in the California courts, she was quoted as saying, "We just own a little box factory in Mascota, *Jalisco*". I thought at the time, "Box factory? Makes boxes to ship drugs in!"

After he was convicted for his direct involvement in the kidnapping, torture, and murder of Enrique Camarena, Sr., our DEA agent, I had the opportunity to meet Mrs. de Zuno at a social gathering in the mountains near Mascota. She was a very pretty, pleasant woman and seemed to be very popular at the party.

I never saw their box factory, but we did buy gasoline for our car at their Pemex station outside of Mascota. I would not have known it belonged to him had I not asked for a receipt. It listed the owner as Ruben Zuno Arce. I wondered how it would look when the accountant at the Embassy saw that the consular agent in Puerto Vallarta was buying gas from the United States' most despicable Mexican criminal at the time.

Automobiles were not furnished to all consular personnel in Mexico. Most of the top officials had State Department owned vehicles, but the majority of us bought in Mexico or drove in from the United States.

Mexico's Exterior Relations Department granted us diplomatic plates for our cars, mainly to exempt us from having to pay exorbitant annual automobile taxes. The plates were subtle enough to not attract undue attention, but they did have the word 'consular' printed at the bottom where the state name ordinarily would be.

Changing an automobile license plate in Mexico is not a casual chore. I don't know how it is in the US or elsewhere these days, but if you sell a car, the plates don't stay with the car. Liability, you know. You don't want the car you sold last week being used in a bank robbery or worse, and the license plate traced back to you. When you sell a car in Mexico, you literally remove the plate, take it with you, along with the buyer, to the office of the state treasurer where he notes the transfer of title of the vehicle, and you are relieved of any future liability.

In my case, I wasn't selling our car, but I was changing license plates. I presented the tax collector with the car title, old plates, my driver's license, official identification, and the new plates. That threw him a curve! He had never seen diplomatic plates before. He gave me the sign; forefinger to thumb, 'Just a minute.'

He conferred with other people in the office, they all thumbed through big manuals, and then he went back to his desk and telephoned somebody. He turned to the wall behind his desk and after a few minutes of almost whispering conversation, he hung up the phone, and smiling broadly, came back to the counter where I was standing.

"*Señora* Consul, forgive me. Your documents will be ready pronto."

When he, at last, handed me the papers I needed to put my new plates on our car, I asked him, "*Señor*, what advantages do I have with these new diplomatic plates?"

"*Señora*, you can park inside the lobby of City Hall if your car can make it up the steps!" So much for DIP plates.

The Transit Department took notice of my new plates and offered me an officially marked parking site on the street near the Consular

Agency. Of course, I jumped at the chance of never having to look for a parking space again, although I usually walked to work. The problem was that the Transit Department had not cleared this with the shop keeper across the street who usually set out chairs or trash buckets in that space to indicate he was expecting a delivery truck that morning.

The only time I remember using that parking space was when Ambassador John Negroponte came to a Businessmen's Conference in Puerto Vallarta. Ambassador Negroponte comes close to basket-ball player proportions. I think he measures in close to seven feet. I knew he would never fit in our car, nor would I be able to park close to the Consular Agency, so the bodyguard changed roles that morning and guarded the parking space. Our friend, Mr. Pepe, offered to drive us in his brand new Ford Airstream.

I never could see that the special license plates gave me any advantage. One night we were driving home and a car behind us began blinking its high beams, on and off. When the opportunity came, the driver pulled alongside us, and yelled out the window, "*Aye, esas placas son de DEA?*" ---Hey, are those DEA license plates?

"No, they're not!" I yelled back.

The next morning we took those plates off, I went back to the state treasurer's office and bought new license plates, which simply identified the car as being registered in the state *Jalisco.*

As many different recreational drugs that are available in Mexico, the laws are tough on the user. California laws were very lenient on a marijuana user. He usually got his hands slapped and maybe even paid a small fine if caught with more than the makings for a joint or two. Our surfing, teen-age spring-breakers were often surprised when they found themselves in the slammer after sharing a cigarette with a friend on the beach. One policeman told me he sat in some of the restaurants along the Malecon, and watched young tourists passing packages of cocaine from mouth to mouth as they kissed.

I had always been curious about why such a to-do was made about what looked like a harmless unfiltered cigarette. I had been smoking a long time, but always stuck to brand name filters.

Many years ago, maybe back in the 60's, my fishing partner, Girl Scout Troop Leader partner, bestest of best friends, Barbara, and I came to Puerto Vallarta on a Girls Only vacation. We had no sooner than plopped our suitcases down in Casa Rebeca, when she said, "Do I ever have a surprise for you!"

"What in the world…?"

"I have two marijuana cigarettes stashed in my purse!"

"Get out of here! How could you possibly dare go through Customs with marijuana on you?" I cried. "You're as ignorant as I am about that stuff. You don't know what would happen to us! We can do enough damage to ourselves with Margaritas. Go to the bathroom right now and flush it down the commode! Now! Go!"

Unenthusiastically, she went into the bathroom, and flushed away our dreams. Not even when she was dying with cancer, and in great pain, would she even think of smoking marijuana. I have heard that it can help ease the hurt, but she wouldn't try it. I did. One. Or at least, part of one.

We were at several parties where chocolate brownies, laced with marijuana were served, but the host always advised us of the ingredients before we took one. My neighbor invited me to his house one evening for a neighborhood pot-luck party. I made my favorite shrimp dip and took it over. That kind of pot-luck was not what he had in mind at all. He brought out a shoe box with several half-smoked roaches in it, and offered the contents to the small group. The guests picked through the butts and chose the length they wanted to smoke. Fortunately, I was not the only one who declined. I decided it was time to make my adieu before the pungent smoke drifted down to the street below where the foot policemen were strolling through the neighborhood.

My time did come eventually. There was a lonely beach named Majahuitas, south of town, yet north of Yelapa.

There's another totally different story, which can stand on its own and will be told someday. Cathy and Von Rohr raised a son there in the jungle. That kid is now on the teaching staff of George Washington University in St. Louis. His specialty is visual communication.

Cathy and son, Enrique, were vacationing in the United States, but she had told Joni Blake she could use her beach house at any time. Joni was secretary to John Huston, the film director, who put Puerto Vallarta on the map. John had built his isolated compound on Las Caletas, the next beach north of Mahajuitas. Joni invited Jean Violet and us to spend the week-end at Majahuitas with her.

Jean had owned an art gallery in Puerto Vallarta for more years than most of us can remember. In fact, her gallery was one of the first to open here. I'm told that galleries open in Puerto Vallarta like Mexican restaurants in the United States; here today, gone tomorrow.

We bought a bag of ice, grabbed a handful of candles, packed a few essentials, and drove to Boca de Tomatlan to hop a ride on a *panga* to Majahuitas.

Cathy was not the only person living in this secluded cove, but hers was the only house visible. She is now a highly respected artist, whose work reflects the many years she lived where her closest neighbors were the parrots, iguanas and sand crabs. The beach could have been right out of a Robinson Crusoe movie.

After a quick swim in the ocean, and a change of clothes, we were ready for another *panga* ride over to Las Caletas. John had invited us to have lunch with him and his house guest, Jack Nicholson. John could have been Jack's father-in-law, but he wasn't. The kids split up housekeeping before they ever got married. When John was at his Las Caletas hide-a-way, he always dressed in formal native garb. That was long, white cotton muslin pants, usually rolled up to mid calf, a pullover shirt of the same material, split from the neck down to about mid chest, *huarache* sandals or no shoes at all.

Somebody on watch must have advised him of our arrival, because before our boatman cut the motor, and we were being washed into shore by the waves, we could see him coming down the path from the main house of his compound. Two young natives were walking by his side, and in that booming Noah voice of his, we could hear him yelling, "Bring 'em in over here!" He directed the young men to wade into the shallows, and grab our boat to steady it while we landed on the sand. What a gentleman!

We crossed the sandy beach, and went up the path to the biggest palm frond thatched roofed building in sight. This was the dining room, reading room, living room, greeting room, and gathering room. Perhaps this is what is meant when interior decorators talk about the 'great room'. It was.

We were introduced to Jack and Her.

I knew about Her, but I had never met her before. I had been told she was somewhat eccentric, to the point of being psychologically impaired. In fact, I had known about Her since the late 60's when John and his fifth wife (whom he always referred to as "The Crocodile") were living in The Macuas Building on Amapas Street. Her was their live-in maid and baby-sitter.

I have no idea what happened, but one night Wifey got so angry she threw as much furniture as she could lift out the fifth floor window of the condo building. Then she packed her bags, the baby, and left town: leaving John and Her to live happily ever after.

Her was seated, curled up in a chair in a dark corner of the reading end of the room. Actually, I think Joni introduced us. I put out my arm to shake hands with her, and with a disdainful smile on her face, she slowly offered her arm up from the chair to meet my hand. I jerked back in horror and let out a terrified scream when I saw there was a live boa constrictor draped around her extended forearm.

Bill Reed called her simply Maid or The *Alacran* (scorpion). Even dear, sweet Gladys Hill (Huston's professional assistant for over twenty years) referred to Her in private conversation as The Bitch. I have heard many others refer to Her as The Gold-Digger, and a few other choice titles. I could add some of my own, but I think I'll just let it go as Her.

We spent a delightful afternoon listening to John and Jack discuss movie production and actors while we gorged ourselves on Archie Alpenia's wonderful Philippine cooking. I don't know where John found Archie, but he made a find when he did. Today Archie's kids carry on the tradition of Archie's fine cooking at the popular El Wok near Los Muertos Beach.

Jack regaled us with stories of Hollywood parties where the main dining table was attractively set with a big silver bowl filled with white powder. He said there was always a small silver spoon in the bowl to use to serve the powder out onto the tabletop. Blades were provided for lining the powder up into a straight line, and plastic drinking straws stood in a silver tumbler.

On another table might be a tray of neatly rolled non-filter cigarettes. He told of ornately designed pipes from far-away oriental places, and he described how to tell a good quality resin from a bad one. He said he was familiar with almost every hallucinogenic drug on the market, but he had never shot heroin or chewed peyote.

Reluctantly, we said our goodbyes, and John sent us back to Majahuitas in his personal *panga*. Her had slithered back into the jungle with her boa, and was not available for the customary farewell.

Back in our own secluded paradise, we gazed at the stars, shared a bottle of red, and reminisced about our afternoon with John Huston, Jack Nicholson and Her.

Mind you, in our minds we were ten thousand miles from civilization, bellies full of good food, and stimulated from unusually enlightening conversation. There were three novices, and one semi-experienced user lying on the beach, listening to the jungle sounds, and no policemen in sight.

I mused aloud, "You know, I can't imagine that Jack knows as much about drugs as he says he does, made as many box-office movies as he has, and never was trashed by the press.

Joni said, "It's a matter of knowing when and where, and who you are with." Who told her? She never even smoked an L&M or Benson Hedges in her lifetime. She even dilutes her white wine with ice cubes!

Jean whispered, "I have a couple of tokes in the house if you're interested."

Interested? I'd been interested since I was almost a teen-ager. I reflected upon Joni's comment of 'where, when and with whom' and decided the moment had arrived.

This was truly a momentous occasion. We folded our towels and solemnly walked back to the house.

Another bottle of red was opened, and two non-filter cigarettes were produced and laid on the table in front of us. Jean lighted one and passed it to me, with the recommendation, "Inhale deeply, hold, and then exhale."

Howard and Joni were staring at us as if we were Martians, waiting for us to sprout horns or communicate with extra-terrestrial beings in an unknown language. I sipped from my glass of wine, puffed a few times on the cigarette in my hand, and finally said to Jean, "This is the most ridiculous thing in the world! I don't feel a thing! I thought bells were supposed to start ringing, and I would feel the melody of music in my bones so strongly that I would waltz with the stars. I don't feel a thing."

She told me, "Wait a bit. It hits different people in different ways."

I kept looking over my shoulder, thinking somebody was gong to come in and direct this scenario. Nothing happened. We sat there and carried on a perfectly normal conversation, just the four of us, sipping on our wine and smoking our non-filters.

Suddenly Jean's face changed. The room changed. Nothing was as it had been. All of a sudden, life was a comedy. To be sitting there in what most people would call paradise, was hilariously funny. Time stood still. Everything about life was detailed and clear. There were no mysteries. It was open ocean, sandy beach, and friends. And it was ecstasy. Jean and I glanced at each other and almost fell off our bar stools laughing. We continued to try to carry on a half-way intelligent conversation, but each time she and I locked eyes, we collapsed into crazy, panty-wetting laughter. Joni and Howard were having a good time, laughing at our laughter. I'd never experienced anything so side-splitting funny in all my life. And never have since then.

The inevitable happened and I had to go to the bathroom. Howard took a kerosene lamp from a table to light my wait down the hall, but when I got off the bar stool; there was no floor underneath my feet. I took steps and I progressed down the hall, but I could feel absolutely nothing under my feet. I had never felt so out of control of my actions before, yet I obviously had motor control. I was moving, and aware that I was moving, but I couldn't feel myself moving. After my visit to the bathroom, I asked Howard to bid the girls good-night for me.

I lay on the bed watching the fireflies flicker through the room, listened to the waves rolling onto the beach and the strange animal noises coming from the jungle. My uppermost thought was: If I ever get down off this cloud, I'll never, ever smoke another joint. Give me a good cold beer, please.

CHAPTER EIGHTEEN

Disappearances

Our newspapers and television screens are filled with stories of abducted children all over the world. We remember grocery bags and milk cartons bearing images of children's faces and details of their disappearance. All too often the mutilated and decomposed remains of these innocent children turn up in a vacant field.

We read about native-born American children ending up in a foreign country; usually transported there by a foreign-born parent, and without the spouse's consent.

In 1954 the United States and about thirty other countries signed what is called The Hague Convention. This Convention was ratified in 1983 to include the Child Abduction clause. Some European, African, and Asian countries refused to sign it. Mexico, the United States and Canada did sign, so that made Child Abduction cases easier to deal with in this part of the world. But all this gubernatorial protection didn't stop baby-trafficking nor child abduction. It is too easy to walk or drive across our borders and get lost in the cracks

In Mexico, the law was usually on our side if we could locate the fleeing parent and child.

Airlines based in Mexico, Canada and the United States require an affidavit signed by the non-accompanying parent, or by both parents if the child is under eighteen years of age and traveling alone.

Mexican men have requested my help in locating, and bringing home, their Mexican wife and children living illegally in the United States. Although

I may feel sorry for the man, there isn't much I can do to help him. They're lost in the cracks in Los Angeles, Chicago or someplace north.

It gets sticky if an American mother decides to leave the Mexican father and go back home with their baby. It gets even stickier if the American woman is married to the Mexican father. However, the Mexican child custody rulings are similar to the United States' rulings, meaning that the mother is usually favored. You gotta be a mean, bad mama to lose yo' baby.

The story is different if the American parent leaves his American partner, married or not, and takes their child into a foreign country.

Luigi Calabrese is one such case I remember.

The kidcaptor usually leaves a paper trail that can be followed and the empty-armed parent has a pretty good idea where his child is.

The Calabreses were Americans from Boston, and although they had a new baby, they were on the outs with each other. Luigi worked in Time-Share Puerto Vallarta while Angela went back home to have the baby. The baby was three months old when Luigi paid a visit to Angela and decided little Luigi should live in Puerto Vallarta. I don't know how he made it all the way from Boston to Puerto Vallarta without being stopped, but he did.

Angela and her sister flew into town and came to see me. She had gambled that Luigi had brought the baby back to the condo where he had been living. She was right. The baby was being taken care of well. Luigi had hired round-the-clock baby-sitters and none of them would allow Angela near the baby.

The Calabreses were married, but with a divorce pending in Boston, so no legal custodian had been established. In cases like this, nine times out of ten, somebody is illegally in the country, so I went probing in the immigration office.

The baby hadn't been registered as a tourist when Luigi brought him across the border. That made him illegally in the country. Luigi, Sr. didn't have working papers either. The immigration officials were only too happy to see that mother and child were reunited and daddy paid a handsome fine to get his papers in order. Case closed.

Mrs. Dawson, Catherine's mother, called me from Dallas. Her story was a sad one. Catherine's ex-husband, James, had brought their two children, Kurt and Cassandra, to Mexico with Catherine's signed Child Permit to Travel. Catherine thought they were coming to the beach for the weekend. That weekend lasted over six months.

Kurt and Cassandra were excited about their trip and had promised their teachers to give a full report to their respective classes upon their return. When time came for them to fly back home, James told the kids he had taken a job selling time-share, and all three of them would be staying in Puerto Vallarta.

Naturally, Catherine was alarmed when her children were not returned to her as promised. She knew their airline tickets had read they were going to Puerto Vallarta, but she had no clue where they might be staying. Looking back, I'm surprised the State Department was not contacted at that point, but nobody was.

Catherine and her mother worked with a travel agency in Dallas, calling every hotel and motel in Puerto Vallarta to no avail. James had moved them into an apartment and they slipped through the crack.

According to what the children later told their mother, they had begged James to call her. They wanted to go home, but unless he signed a Child Permit to Travel for them, no airline would allow them to board a plane. These were kids nine and eleven years old and they were in a foreign country with their father, but without their mother. They didn't know where to turn for help.

James enrolled both children in the American School and they were able to make friends with some of the other children. They finally decided to tell one of the American teachers why their mother could not come to Parent-Teacher meetings. That teacher did not call me, but she did call Catherine. Children and mother were re-united by phone, and Catherine was assured they were well, and she learned where they were living and got a phone number for them. She could talk to the children whenever she wanted, but James would not allow them to return to Dallas.

This was about the time Mrs. Dawson first called me. Catherine had made her plans to come to Puerto Vallarta and kidnap her children back. She asked if I could help. I was apprehensive about getting involved in a kidnapping, but I was willing. I suggested that Catherine bring as much evidence as she had that the children were her natural issue and that she had legal custody of them. I told the grandmother to instruct Catherine to get the children out of the apartment on some pretext, if she could, and come see me.

It was easier to do that I would have thought. Catherine flew in, went to the apartment, saw her children and even spent the night with them. She convinced James she was merely visiting to make sure they were alright. He took the kids to school the next day as if it were the normal thing to do and left Catherine on her own until he would return with Kurt and Cassandra.

Catherine had managed to have time alone with her children the night before and they made their plans. She gave Kurt money so that his teacher could call a taxi for him and Cassandra to come back to the apartment. She used her time in the vacant apartment to rummage through clothes, and pack a small bag for each child. She found where James was hiding their three passports. She took them all.

My plan was to write a letter to the immigration officials at the Puerto Vallarta airport, copy to the airline manager and immigration officials in Dallas.

The three appeared at the Consular Agency around ten o'clock. Their flight was due to leave at twelve. We had no time to lose. I made photo copies of divorce papers, court rulings, birth certificates, even newspaper clippings that Catherine had brought with her, which described how James had violated his visiting privileges. I put the copies into separate envelopes addressed to the travel officials along with the letter I had written on American Consular Agency letterhead. I even stamped my signature with the official embossed seal. Sometimes official-looking paper work throws the most determined non-cooperative bureaucrap off track,

As I dated my letter, I realized the day was May 10th. That is Mexico's official Mothers' Day! Can you get a better gift than to be re-united with your children?

Catherine left James' passport with me. Eventually, he came to me to report its loss. It was a pleasure to be able to tell him that someone had recovered the passport and turned it in at the Consular Agency.

It was not uncommon for teen-agers to become separated from their parents while vacationing here. Girls meet boys on the beach in the daytime. They make plans to join up for dinner and dancing at one of our many discothèques and the clock stands still. They dance the night away, walk the beach hand-in-hand at dawn and maybe even stop for breakfast before going back to the hotel where the parents are staying.

In the meantime, the frantic parents are convinced their kid has been kidnapped, murdered or in jail. A couple of quick phone calls can rule out murder or arrest, but kidnapping is more difficult. Usually by the time I had gotten a verbal description of the missing youngster, including what type of clothes he or she had been wearing, the wandering one showed up at the hotel. "Just having a good time, Mom," she declares.

Angry spouses who walk out, slam the door and disappear are a different issue. They're usually easy to find. Most adults carry their own credit cards. If they go to another hotel and register in their own name, and they usually do, they've left a paper trail. There is such a thing as a Hotel-Motel Association in most of our towns. I was on a friendly basis with the folks who worked in that office. They could check out all the hotels in an hour or so and find out if Jane Doe was in a different hotel than the one she originally registered in with her husband John.

The problem was I couldn't tell John Doe where his wife was. I could tell him she was safe, unharmed and would contact him when she got good and ready. Any more information than that, and I would have been violating the Privacy Act.

Others were more serious. Dan and Marsha Ortiz were newly-married Americans from San Antonio who were honey-mooning in our city. One of the high-points of their trip had been suggested by their travel agent. "You can't miss Lopez' Paradise Restaurant!" she had told them.

They rented a Jeep and off they went for a day in Paradise. The spot is enchanting. The month was October. The rains had polished the green foliage to a sparkle; the summertime roaring river had quieted down to a friendly flow. There were mammoth boulders in the river, causing the water to make small wading pools. You can cross the river stepping from one stone to a puddle of water and on to another stone, and then into a wading pool. Then there is a drop of about fifteen feet and you see a swirling eddy of water. If you go down the river from rock to rock, you can dive into a pool of calm water, but if you fall from up high into the eddy, we probably won't ever find you. There are caves along the river walls where a body can be sucked into, a boulder tumbled over the opening and there you lie forever.

Marsha was snapping photographs with her new camera and she wanted Dan to pose for her on a rock jutting out above the deep eddy. Arms raised into the air, his blue t-shirt with the caption, San Antonio Spurs, printed across the front, showing off his muscles, he was ready for the shot when he held up his hand and said, "Wait a minute! I think I hear something down here!"

Marsha turned to one side to lay the camera on her beach towel, looked up and didn't see Dan. He had totally disappeared. Gone!

The police advised me of this case. I went to see Marsha in her hotel room, which was supposed to have been her honey-moon suite. She had a hard-side suitcase open on a luggage rack. There were lighted candles surrounding the suitcase. The inside lid had a print of the

Virgin of Guadalupe glued to it. Marsha had brought her altar with her and she was praying for her Danny.

Aurelio Vazquez, my friend who used to operate a restaurant on Morelos Street, and who used to feed my folks who didn't have money for food, was also an expert diver. More than once he swam that treacherous river looking for bodies, which had disappeared in avalanches of roaring waters. He found some, but he didn't find Dan Ortiz.

Marsha was convinced there was a conspiracy going on. She couldn't let go of Dan's last words, "Wait a minute. I think I hear something down here!"

In her grief, she was sure that Dan had been abducted and was being held captive in a cave where he had no control over his senses. In a way, she was right.

Two of Dan's brothers flew down to be with Marsha. They visited with the police, newspaper reporters, waiters at the restaurant, natives who lived along the river and me. There was no clue as to what had happened to Dan.

The brothers offered a reward of $2,000 dollars to anybody furnishing information, which would lead to the recovery of Dan's body. They left photographs of him with the police and me.

The word spread through the community that Dan had taken out a $100,000 dollar, double indemnity life insurance policy shortly before he and Marsha were married. She was the beneficiary, but she couldn't collect since she couldn't prove he was dead.

It was in March of the following year when two young Mexican boys decided to do some early morning fishing along the Horcones River. They were picking their way down the river, stepping from boulder to boulder. Both boys screamed when their flashlights revealed what appeared to be a human body barely covered by the water. It was lodged between two huge rocks. The frightened boys ran home to their parents.

The father of one of the boys reported to the police department that they had found what might be a body in the river. The police investigated, the body was brought up and taken to a funeral home. Ignacio called me.

"I think we have found Dan Ortiz' body," he said. He told me how the boys had been surprised on their early morning fishing trip.

I asked, "What makes you think it's Ortiz? Does he look like the pictures the police have?"

"The body is badly decomposed. You have to remember he has been under water for six months. He's wearing a t-shirt, which is torn, but I can make out San Antonio Spurs printed on it."

I phoned one of Dan's brothers in Texas to notify him of this latest development. He promised to be on the next flight out of San Antonio.

Normally, a decomposed body was buried in the local cemetery immediately after positive identification had been made. However, Dan's family wanted to ship his remains back home. This presented a problem.

We shipped bodies back to the United States on a routine basis, and the procedure was fairly simple. There are some parts of Mexico where morticians don't do embalming and there is a general rule that a body must be disposed of within twenty-four hours of death. It is also rare that you find a make-up artist working in a mortuary in Mexico. Ignacio had spent some time in Dallas learning about embalming and cadaver presentation.

None of the tricks of his trade could be used in this case. Any body being shipped anywhere on any airline has to be placed in a hermetically sealed box, so the decaying odor doesn't reach the passengers. This time the odor from the decomposition was too powerful to be sealed in.

We didn't have a crematory in Puerto Vallarta then. The closest one was in Guadalajara. The Ortiz brothers were willing to pay for the added expense of transporting Dan to the crematory. They would fly to Guadalajara, pick up the ashes and return to San Antonio. They wanted to meet the young boys who had found Dan in the river.

Before all these plans were finalized, Marsha phoned me and said, "Tell them I want his gold wedding ring back."

When I called Ignacio to tell him to be sure to give the wedding ring to one of the brothers, he said very softly, "There is no ring, Jenny. He doesn't have any fingers."

"No fingers? What do you mean? No fingers? What happened to them?"

"He's been under water six months. They either rotted off or the fish might have eaten them."

"How am I going to explain to Marsha Ortiz that her husband has no fingers?" I cried.

"The brothers already know," he replied.

Of course the media had followed this case from the day Dan disappeared. I'm always amazed how reporters manage to know what's going on, and where to be at the right moment. The day after the Ortiz brothers left Puerto Vallarta, *Vallarta Opina* ran an article with a picture of them handing checks of $1,000 dollars each to the boys who found Dan. When the reporter asked them what they intended to do with the money, one was quoted as saying, "I'm going to buy my mama a refrigerator!" The other boy chimed in, "I'm going to get mine a new stove!"

That river ate too many folks to talk about. There was a young girl named Madeline who was vacationing with a group of her college classmates. She simply disappeared from the group. Nobody saw her fall, didn't hear her cry out, nor see her body floating down the river. Aurelio and his divers even put nets across the mouth of the river where it emptied into the ocean at Boca de Tomatlan, but her body was never recovered. We assume she lies in a wet cave.

When I think about the on-going investigations made in recent years of spring-break teenagers disappearing in foreign countries, I'm surprised that so little was done in trying to find Madeline.

It was her boyfriend who reported her disappearance to me. He brought me a picture of her which I kept on file as long as I was in the office. However, I don't recall a big to-do being made about her disappearance. I do recall reporting her disappearance to her parents, but nobody flew down to push further investigation. Maybe, just maybe, she didn't disappear after all.

The only other person, who totally disappeared, never to be found again, was Joseph Swaggart. His disappearance still remains a mystery.

Joe worked as a flight attendant for a Texas-based airline. Houston was the hub of this international airline and Joe kept an apartment there. One of the perks for working for an airline was he was able to fly free to anyplace his airline serviced. He and his girl friend, Linda, chose to come to Puerto Vallarta.

I don't think Joe and Linda were anything more than good friends who worked for the same airline. They both registered under their own name in the same room in the Sheraton Hotel. Linda called me almost twenty-four hours after she had last seen Joe.

"He put on his walking shorts and tennis shoes, picked up his passport and money clip from dresser top and said, 'I'm going out for a pack of cigarettes. I'll be back in a minute.' That was about five o'clock yesterday afternoon," she told me.

Linda had already notified the hotel manager that Joe was missing and by the time I got to the hotel, a full-scale investigation was underway. I was reminded of some of the breaking news stories I see on television these days. Federal policemen were on the scene because a beach in Mexico is considered to be in the Federal Zone. City police were there as well as the state police. The hotel had its own security squad, which knew every nook and cranny around the hotel. They assured me they had even checked out the drain system. Joe was not to be found.

I asked Linda if they had quarreled. She said, "No, we had been at the pool most all day and we were planning on going into town for dinner last night. He just never came back with his cigarettes."

I thought perhaps he had taken a different flight back to Houston. Since he had free travel on the airline he worked for, I couldn't imagine he would pay for a ticket on another airline. However, some airlines have reciprocal agreements. We checked that out also. There was no record that a Joseph Swaggart departed Puerto Vallarta on any airline. Linda didn't know how much money Joe had with him. He had left his key ring on the dresser along with his airline voucher home and his tourist card. He had only taken his passport and money clip.

Joe's distraught mother and sister flew in from Providence, Rhode Island. They brought photographs and they talked with all the investigators. Joe's mother let it drop that he owed Internal Revenue Service $10,000 dollars in back taxes. Bad as IRS might be, ten grand is no reason to do a deep six, but we couldn't find Joe.

Joe's mother offered $5,000 dollars for information leading to the whereabouts of her son. Linda and Joe's family returned to their homes with the mystery unsolved.

This case was kept alive in the media with everybody hoping we would find another body or a live Joe would appear. Neither happened.

One day my old friend Elena Gollum called. She asked, "By the way, Jenny, have you ever thought of contacting a psychic?"

"Well, no, Nena. But why would I contact a psychic? What about?"

"I know a woman who can sometimes find lost things. She might be able tell you something about that missing airline attendant."

Elena and I had played this game before. We had actually solved a murder a few years back. We had almost the same dream about a German man killing his wife with a kitchen knife. It was spooky that we had both dreamed about the couple the night she was murdered and we had dreamed that he did it. They had a clothing store on the corner of Constitucion and Basilio Badillo Streets. She was the seamstress, and made dresses, shorts and shirts from a special batik fabric. Elena and I dreamed of exactly how she was dressed when she was killed. The man was questioned and released, but later was convicted of her murder.

With this unusual experience behind us, I thought her idea of seeing a physic might be valid.

"Will you go with me?" I asked.

"I'd love to. I'll call her now."

It wasn't long before Elena called me back.

"Pick me up at my house. She lives nearby."

We went to a beauty salon on Jacarandas Street. The woman was a hairdresser and lived behind her salon. I expected to see her dressed in a long robe with a turban on her head. She was as normal looking as you and I. There wasn't even a glass ball anywhere in sight. There was nobody else in the salon. She invited us to sit as she reached for the phone on a nearby table. She lifted the receiver from its cradle and laid it aside.

"Now tell me about the missing man," she said.

I told her everything I knew and tried to remember details Linda, Joe's mother and sister had told me. She folded her hands in her lap, motioned for Elena and me to be quiet and she closed her eyes.

"He is not dead," she told us. "He is happy. He is out in the country. I don't see any buildings or cars, but I see lots of trees. He can see for miles around him. He can see cows grazing on green grass, but they seem to be far away. He is happy and he is smiling. He is wearing dungarees, boots and a warm jacket. The weather is chilly, but not cold. He is happy."

She opened her eyes and said, "I don't know where he is, but he's not dead."

We thanked her for giving us the reading and left her still seated.

"What do you make of that?" I asked Elena when we got outside.

"She says he's not dead," she said off-handedly.

"From her description of his clothes and surroundings, I would say he's definitely not in Puerto Vallarta either."

"What are you going to tell his family?" She asked.

"I really don't know. Maybe it's best not to say anything to them. If I tell them what we've done, they'll either think we're crazy or building hope for his eventual return. I think I'll just wait and see how it plays out."

Several weeks passed and one day a FeeBee showed up. He said he was investigating the Swaggart case. From what he told me about his results, it sounded like our hair-curling psychic had better vision than we had hoped.

Joe's post office box gave up some interesting secrets. Master Charge and American Express vouchers revealed that he had recently bought a small Yamaha motorbike, hiking boots, denim pants and a fleece-lined waterproof jacket. None of these items were in his apartment in Houston. His airline attendant uniform was hanging in the closet, but very little other clothing was found. A television and radio were in the apartment along with several cases of audio cassettes, but no tape player.

The airline's crew scheduling records showed that Joe had spent six weeks on temporary duty in Australia the previous year. His name never appeared on a passenger manifest of any international airline serving Melbourne or Sydney.

I asked the FBI agent, "Do you ever work with psychics in your investigations?"

"No, I don't. Some investigators do, but I don't believe in them," he replied.

I didn't tell him we had consulted with one. I never learned if Joe Swaggart ever surfaced or not. I like to think he's herding sheep on a Yamaha somewhere in the outback and that he has made friends with the aborigines. I hope he wrote his mama.

CHAPTER NINETEEN

RED, WHITE AND BLUE

I can't think of anybody who gets more goose bumps than I do when I hear patriotic music. Well, maybe Poor Judy or Mean Pat do. Poor Judy used to wear glasses, which would darken when she got out in the sunlight and you never could really see the tears in her eyes. You could tell she was trying to control her emotions by the little quiver at the corner of her mouth, and the hair on her arms would stick up.

Nobody has bigger eyes than Mean Pat and she didn't wear tinted glasses. During the playing of Stars Spangled Banner was one time she kept her mouth shut. She stood there, straight and tall and let the tears run. After the anthem was over, she would pull out a wad of tissue, wipe her face and swear, "Damn! It's hot out here!"

While Phil Ober was consular agent here, we were always invited to La Banana Restaurant for dinner on July 4th. This was the way Gustavo Flores, the owner, saluted his American patrons. Of course the invitation was made to Phil and he extended it to a select few.

There weren't a lot of people to choose from when making out a summertime guest list. Eadie and Mac McMurtry who were a bare two inches taller than midgets, Dr. Raul Silva, and his wife, Lynne. She was the one who always wore a triple strand fake-pearl choker to hide her draping aging neck. She usually slept in her plate before the evening was over. Then there was Thaddeus Killar and The Doctor, Dick Reid. Dick, who was once quoted as saying, "A day without Thad is like a week in paradise." Genevieve and Sean Stanford were always part of the group. Gen's San Francisco wardrobe was circa 1940 and Sean usually followed Lynne Silva's sleeping habits, if he didn't fall out of his chair first. Mayo and Bill Warren brought in more San Francisco influence. Come to think of it, we were the only real foreigners in this group. Everybody else was from California. Jack Wilhoit, Ralph Todesca and Mary Shaw, when she was in town, rounded out our group.

These were truly boring parties. We sat lined up at a long table. The music was so loud you could only talk with the person directly in front of you and to either side. The food was your typical tough, grilled steak, rice, mashed beans and a dab of guacamole with the stale tostado sticking in it.

I leaned over to Eadie McMurtry one night and whispered, "I'm never coming to one of the Fourth of July dinners again!"

She returned my whisper, "Oh, yes you will and so will the rest of us. As long as Phil invites us, we'll all be here."

There were no more invitations to La Banana after Phil died.

He died in September 1981 and if I recall correctly, a small group got together in 1982 on the beach near Vista del Sol condos. We were three Americans, one Mexican, one Canadian, and two half Mexicans. The two half Mexicans were Juan and Mauricio, sons of Judy de Galeana and Nicole de Vazquez. It rained.

I don't remember this, but Pat Flanery has a memory like an elephant. She says we had a quiet dinner at Bill and Jo Skinner's beach house in 1983. It rained.

Jo was a marvelous cook and Bill was born behind a bar. He never remembered anybody's name. He called all men Stud, and all women, Tomato. He and Jo had owned a restaurant in San Bernardino. He said it was good business to greet the Studs and Tomatoes that way. It made them feel special, and they spent accordingly.

We celebrated in grand style in 1984 at Ken and Pat Flanery's beach house. There was a visiting US Navy ship in port, and of course, that made everything even more red, white and blue. Bell-bottomed trousers quickly changed into bare-bottomed sailors. The beer flowed freely and after all, they were on R&R. Rugged and Risqué.

I was extra puffed up that day. Ambassador John Gavin had authorized, let's say given an order, that I should be allowed a paid consular assistant. After working the murder case at the golf course on Easter morning, I had been summoned to Guadalajara to give an account of exactly what had transpired, and at what time each event took place. After my debriefing, Ambassador Gavin asked me, "Now, what can we do for you, Jenny?"

"Mr. Ambassador, I need an assistant. My friends have been helping me carry the load, but I need full-time help."

He turned to his second-in-command at the Embassy and said, "Mr. Lane, see to it that Jenny is budgeted an assistant."

Lane replied, "Mr. Ambassador, Mrs. Allen in Budget and Finance will never authorize that."

The Ambassador looked at Larry Lane with surprise on his face, and in his eloquent speaking voice said, "Mr. Lane, I did not make a request. I gave an order."

I'll always love John Gavin for this. Although he was of Mexican descent and spoke fluent Spanish, when President Ronald Reagan appointed him as Ambassador, the Mexican media drug him through the coals. Spokespersons for the Mexican government claimed he was not a diplomat; nothing but a movie actor.

Gavin's come-back was, "That's not true. I've got fifty-seven movies to prove I'm not an actor." Behind his back, he was always called, Ambassador Guapo Juan. Handsome John.

Jackie had actually been working with me over a year, and I had been paying her salary from my own pocket, but this 4th of July was her first official day at work. It rained.

I'm drawing a total blank about 1985 and '86, but we really strutted in 1987. The American School had been built the year before, and it seemed fitting that American Independence Day should be celebrated there.

Consulate Generals and Embassies have Entertainment Funds, which are used for flag-waving occasions. If a consul general wants to invite the governor out to lunch, he can turn in a voucher and be reimbursed. Consular Agencies don't have such funds and we needed money.

Burt Hixson had recently remodeled his home, Villa Verano, and instead of throwing away his old furniture, he passed some on to his friends. I was the new owner of a big dining table. I invited a group of "tank thinkers" to sit at our new table.

Michael Hepburn, Howard, Judy de Galeana, Nancy de Almaraz, Steve Wilson, Helen Jones, Ron Walker, and I put our thinking caps on. We didn't want to charge an entry fee, but we didn't have any seed money to buy refreshments that we could sell. We decided that a few of us would ante up $100 dollars for sodas, beer, hot dogs, and watermelons. If we made any money at the party, we would divvy it up afterwards. If we didn't, we'd have a good time.

Steve and Ron Walker were in charge of games and activities. We wanted as many Mexican families to come as Americans, and we thought the children would enjoy playing organized games, such as spoon races, burlap bag races, and balloon dancing. The most popular with the big kids was tossing horse-shoes.

Judy and Angelo were in charge of the refreshment stand. Nancy arranged for the hot dog man. Ron was the only one with a pick-up truck, so he offered it for hauling our supplies, with Steve or Howard driving. Michael would deliver invitations to the dignitaries. He also was in charge of publicity and entertainment. All I had to do was worry about the official ceremony, and if the mayor would sit by the chief of police, or by the state district attorney. We were set. We had a nest egg and chores to do. The show would go on!

The American School was not what you see today. There were three classrooms, two toilets, and a tiny office for Gerald Selitzer, the director. A new concrete pad had recently been poured, which would become the volley ball court. We had no trees or grass yet. A few bushes were scattered about, but everything still looked pretty raw.

We were trying to get the school accredited as an Overseas American School. When I had asked Consul General Irvin Rubenstein to give us a recommendation for the school, he responded, "That's a waste of time. It'll never happen. The State Department won't ever fund any more Overseas Schools!"

Gerry and his wife, Kathy, wouldn't be celebrating with us that year. They were off to Washington, D.C. on a mission.

Incidentally, the American School Puerto Vallarta is now an accredited Overseas American School.

We had another committee meeting. It seemed that all was well under control until someone asked, "Where are the flag poles?" Oh, no! We can't hoist a flag without a flag pole!

I learned a lot about flag-waving that year. I knew several ironmongers, but their prices were higher than the flag pole would be. I mentioned this to my friends, Miguel and Bea Escontria. Mike said, "Let me take care of that. I know a man who'll give me a good price." And he did.

We had to have two poles; one for the American flag, and the other for the Mexican flag. It doesn't matter how tall a flag pole is as long as the flag doesn't touch the ground, but the American flag must fly at least one inch below that of the host country.

Part of the official ceremony was to present lapel pins of the American and Mexican flags to Judy, Jackie and Steve Wilson, as a token of my appreciation for standing by my side through some difficult times.

A vice-consul was visiting from Guadalajara so I chose him to put the pin on Judy. I don't know why I came up with the idea of actually pinning the lapel pin in place. It would have been simple enough to hand it to them, but no, I wanted flourish! I pinned Steve. No problem there. Mayor Aurelio Rodriguez was given the honor of pinning little Jackie. His face turned red and his hands trembled as he looked for a way to pin the lapel of her low-cut strapless sun dress. Give the man credit. At least he didn't stick her in the *teta*.

Sean Hennessey was a fugitive from justice in the United States, but we didn't know it. He was in Puerto Vallarta ripping off, among others, Andres Famania at his restaurant on Los Muertos Beach, but he was a great entertainer and loved his flag. He dressed in his Uncle Sam costume, hooked up his special sound system and sang. He sang, we danced and it rained. Oh, how it rained!

We managed to cover some of the tables with tarps, but it looked as if the one over the dignitaries' table would fall on them any minute! Before disaster struck, somebody had sense enough to poke a broom handle up from underneath so the water ran off to the sides.

The party was a success. While the clean-up crew slipped and slid around in the mud as they loaded the uncut watermelons back into Ron's pick-up, Michael and I danced.

We danced our last dance in the rain.

Andres Famania would have his day in a Boston court confronting Sean with his Mexican shyster dealings in January of the following year. The prosecuting attorney met Andres at the airport with a heavy overcoat. It snowed.

For the next few years we played our anthems at Mismaloya Beach. Dr. John was our official medico for these events, and he actually used one Band-Aid on a scrapped knee one time. Robin Lloyd and John Boyd, his accomplice, were filming our celebrations. They even caught a shot of our flag being hoisted upside down!

Reese Oakley, a former manager of Piggly Wiggly grocery stores in the United States had come to town, and he was working for the well-known, and growing, Gutierrez Rizo grocery chain. Mexico had recently entered into GATT, and Tina Gutierrez had hired Reese for the main store on 5th of Febrero Street. His primary job was to find out what the gringo community wanted. He carried a notepad and pencil in his hand and asked all of us, "What would you like to see in this grocery store?"

"Wow! Reese! Get me some Aunt Jemima's corn meal mix, horseradish, good dill pickles, Dijon mustard...my list is long. I'm also looking for some good hot dogs for our Fourth of July picnic."

"Why don't you talk to Tina and see if she will donate hot dogs for the party?"

"Donate? You've got to be kidding! I can't do that!"

"Then I'll ask her," Reese promised.

The Gutierrez Rizo family-operated corner grocery store, and especially Tina, became the official silent promoters of our Independence Day celebrations and Poor Judy Galeana and I became the Cole Slaw Queens. We still carry the title.

Thank Goodness, we never got into baked beans or potato salad, but we did a number on cole slaw. Judy had a new Cuisinart food processor, so we decided to apply our culinary skills in her house. She bought the ingredients, and I went over to help her with the complicated mastery of pushing certain buttons to chop, grind or grate. My Poor Dear Judy didn't know anything. All she could do was read the instructions to me. I knew machinery from inside to out. We skinned the onions, scrapped those carrots, sliced the cabbage into manageable quarters, and punched them into the food processor. All hell broke loose!

We had cabbage, carrots and onions flying over Judy's kitchen like confetti in Times Square on New Year's Eve. Judy didn't read me the part about putting the lid on before pressing the button.

In the fall of 1990, Martin Dreiwitz, conductor and founder of the Long Island Youth Orchestra visited Puerto Vallarta. He came to see me with a proposal. His orchestra had been making summer tours since 1971. They had traveled the United States, Europe, Malaysia, Japan, Korea, Latin and Central American countries, but had never performed in Mexico. They wanted to come to Puerto Vallarta in the summer of 1991.

"We are an eighty-two instrument orchestra, and we can give as many free performances as you want, but we generally like to limit them to once a day." He continued, "We usually stay in youth hostels, but we're willing to stay any place you can find us."

"Eighty-two, did you say?"

"Plus five adults. We're working on spending money for the group, but would appreciate it if you could get us discounts on food somewhere."

Light bulbs were popping around in my head! I couldn't imagine how we would manage eighty-seven non-paying guests, but I saw a challenge I couldn't ignore. I couldn't remember anything like this had ever happened in Puerto Vallarta before. Just think of what an inspiration this could be for some of our Mexican kids! I nibbled at the hook.

"Can they play The Star Spangled Banner?" I asked.

"Beautifully." He answered.

"Do you think you could teach them to play the Mexican national anthem?" I inquired.

"Without a doubt." Dreiwitz assured me.

"Then how would you like to celebrate the Fourth of July in Puerto Vallarta next year?" I asked.

"We'll be here, drums and all."

He accepted the challenge also, but he had the upper hand on me. He'd been doing this for years, and I was a green-horn at something this big. It was that easy. We shook hands and he walked out, leaving me wondering out loud, "Oh, what have I done now?"

I figured that among Jackie, Luis Guillermo, and all our friends, we could find enough beds for everybody. All of us knew how to smear mayonnaise on a slice of bread. The food might not be gourmet, but they wouldn't starve. After all, we had fed Queen Elizabeth's subjects.

Remember me telling you about the Exception to the Rule when I explained to you about "Time Share"? Well, I phoned those Exceptions.

When I told them what I had done and what I needed, Fernando let out a soft whistle, "Wiiiish, Jenny, that's a Big Time request!"

"Yes, but I've got Big Time buddies too!"

"I'll see what I can do and call you back."

Then I called my friend, Lola Covarrubias, who was Chief of Civil Registry in City Hall, and asked her to check with her folks to see where they thought the performances would do the most good. I asked for help anywhere I could get it.

Consular activities didn't come to a screeching halt simply because we were planning a big party. The 4 D's persisted. People continued to Die, others were Detained; many were Destitute, and a few Disappeared. The calendar moved forward, but we were making progress.

Fernando had called, "We can house them at the condominiums Villa del Mar, and include a Continental breakfast. We'll have to charge for lunch, but we can give them a sandwich, fries and a soda for fifteen pesos each, or $1.50 US."

Lola had reported that the Hotel Sheraton would offer space for one concert and the new shopping mall at Marina Vallarta would be another good spot. Those two places would be far enough separated that people from different areas of town would have the opportunity to hear the Long Island kids play. Luis Wulff and his mom, Nellie, had offered El Dorado Restaurant for the official ceremony, and would have hot dogs and hamburgers at a special price on the 4th.

Marina Vallarta was developing rapidly. Good restaurants opened, and up-scale shops popped up all around. Condos were built. Realtors were doing big business. We even had a yacht club.

Then Lucille Boston blew into town.

Lucille was a lawyer from Los Angeles. She bought one of the biggest units in the Royal Pacific condominiums in Marina Vallarta. She had grandiose ideas, even bigger than mine. Everything about Lucille was big except her tiny miniature French poodle dog. Fifi entertained at Lucille's parties by doing her push-up exercises on a rubber doll. Lucille complained that Fifi was really hard on her toys. She had to replace the doll about once a month.

She came up with the idea of Marina Del Rey in California and Marina Vallarta becoming Sister Marinas.

I have no idea where the Sister Marina program came from, but the Sister City program came about in 1956 when President Dwight Eisenhower proposed the People to People program. Puerto Vallarta has enjoyed a sister relationship with Sta. Barbara, California since 1972, so why not have a Sister Marina?

"It's a great idea, Lucille, but you do the organizing. I have my hands full with the Long Island Youth Orchestra and our Independence Day party," I told her.

"Let's do it on the Fourth of July! That way we'll have one gigantic party!" she exclaimed.

"O.K. Go for it!" I agreed with her.

That's how it came to be that we had so many visitors from California that July. Lucille invited the *Commandante* of our yacht club to Los Angeles and they went to work

Along about the end of May that year Martin Dreiwitz sent me a recorded cassette of his young musicians and I almost fainted. I had no idea what I was listening to. It sounded like a warm-up session of the ompa-ompa band which strolls our streets from time to time. My only thought was, "It's too late to back out now."

By late June we had all our ducks in order. Dreiwitz had made arrangements for ground transportation for his group and instruments through a travel agency. Lucille was responsible for her group's arrival and accommodations. The media was giving us daily write-ups and radio spots on coming events. All seemed to be going well, but I was terrified.

"The main attraction can't play! They'll lose their horns. Nobody will come to the free concerts! The Mexican Navy men will raise our flag upside down again! I'll lose my cue cards for introductions! I'll get sick! I'll faint! I'll have to go the bathroom!" All that and more went through my mind as the clock ticked toward the afternoon of July 1st, the day of their arrival.

For their first night in town, Burt Hixson invited the kids, their adult companions and a few of our hard working Americans for a swim and hamburgers at his gorgeous villa. The Cole Slaw Queens were called back to duty, the cooks at the villa were shoved aside by our own chefs, Lynn Nokes, Marg Tolton, and Missy Case, but the new Queen of the Day was Polly Vicars.

Polly and Husband (his name is Hubert, but she calls him Husband) had their own fishing boat. They went out to the deep two or three times a week, and rarely came back to shore without a blue flag flying, indicating they had their catch for the day. Tuna was plentiful in our bay those days, and what they didn't eat they gave to friends or stored in their freezer. Polly thought we should offer the group tuna burgers also.

"Tuna burgers! That's just what I need now! One of my close friends losing her mind at this crucial time!" I had never heard of tuna burgers before, but those Long Island kids scarffed them down like hot cakes. We had hamburgers left over, but no tuna burgers. I learned something new that day. Tuna makes a "great" burger!

The group was free to run and play during the day, but at 7:30 each evening for the next two days they would be giving their free concerts. The performances were not attended as well as I would have liked, but they were having a good time. One of my biggest fears had been laid to rest. These kids could play! Martin had sent me a lousy tape.

When Howard got up on the morning of the 4th, he found me sitting at our table on the terrace with a pencil in my hand, a full ashtray of cigarette butts, a cup of coffee and a half-empty bottle of Pepto Bismol. I was still working on my introductory speech.

El Dorado Restaurant was packed: stand room only. As the Mexican flag was raised, Martin Dreiwitz brought his baton down with a swift movement of his hand and the Long Island Youth Orchestra played!

Oh, lord, how they played! Played beautifully! Although the horn section and the string section had practiced, they had never played the entire Mexican national anthem together before. Mexican men let the tears run unashamedly down their face.

Our own Red, White and Blue was raised as the orchestra gloriously played The Star Spangled Banner. And what do you think I did? I pulled a wad of tissue from my pocket, wiped my face, and whispered into the microphone, "Damn, it's hot in here!"

Just as I was shuffling my cue cards in order to make introductions, I felt a hand on my shoulder. I turned to see Engineer Fernando Rivera handing me a sealed envelope.

"I want to give you a gift on this special day. The titles are clear. The owners can come back to their condos on Olas Altas Street. My word is good."

I had used my last tissue.

Governor Pete Wilson didn't come, but he sent his representative. We had members from California's Tourist Bureau, Los Angeles County Supervisor, Marina Del Rey's Commander and all their spouses eating hot dogs with us that day. Our mayor proclaimed that at "as of 2:15, July 4th, 1991, Puerto Vallarta and Marina Del Rey are Sister Marinas."

And then it rained…and rained…and rained.

ABOUT THE AUTHOR

JENNY MCGILL and her husband, Howard moved to ¨Puerto Vallarta, Mexico in 1973. She was appointed consular agent by the U.S. State Department in 1982, and spent the next fourteen years in that position.

Upon retirement, the McGills sought out the tranquility of the western Sierra Madres in a small village, Talpa de Allende, *Jalisco*. There she devotes her time to writing, promoting local artists, and gardening. She says, "My love of robin-egg blue skies, breath taking sunsets that only God could paint, and music, which falls softly on my ear, is reason enough to be in Mexico.

Some natives consider Jenny to be more Mexican than a frijol.

Made in the USA
San Bernardino, CA
20 May 2013